THE TRAVELING WILBURYS

THE BIOGRAPHY

BY NICK THOMAS

GUARDIAN EXPRESS MEDIA
Green, Ohio U.S.A.

Library of Congress Cataloging-in-Publication Data
Thomas, Nick

    The Traveling Wilburys: The Biography
    Includes bibliographical references
    ISBN 978-0980056174
    1. Rock music – Bio-bibliography.
    I. Title

Second Printing

We would like to thank the following individuals and organizations: John Mascolo, Mike Olszewski, Cheryl Storey, Andrea Schroeder, the Library and Archives of the Rock and Roll Hall of Fame and Museum, and the Music Library and Sound Recordings Archives at Bowling Green State University. Additionally, we are grateful to all of the individuals who consented to our interview requests.

Please contact the publisher to report any errors or omissions. Organizations and other groups interested in purchasing quantities of this book should contact the publisher.

▶ TABLE OF CONTENTS

▶ INTRODUCTION

The Traveling Wilburys had a short history but a long past. The creation of the group was a fortunate accident, and was the result of an informal recording session within the plain white walls of a cluttered garage. The five seasoned musicians – three of whom were in their 40s – had gathered to assist a former Beatle in writing and recording what was intended as a throwaway B-side track. But for the newly formed group, there was no roadmap, no detailed plan, no record company involvement and no expectation of success.

Nicknamed the Billion Dollar Quintet, the five musical legends could all speak of their own individual achievements, their own musical triumphs, as well as their own extended periods of fan indifference. While Tom Petty's career was at its peak, George Harrison and Roy Orbison were both enjoying newfound glory after long slumps. Bob Dylan, meanwhile, was a strong draw on the concert road but had not had a radio hit for a number of years. Conversely, Jeff Lynne walked away from his longtime band, the Electric Light Orchestra, and had launched a new career as a record producer.

The Traveling Wilburys would release just two albums, both of which were quickly written, recorded and mixed. The group never scored a top-40 hit, but many of their songs like "Handle With Care" and "End Of The Line" became well known and received plenty of radio airplay. The five members never gave interviews as a complete group. Individually, they revealed very little about the recording sessions. And despite their name, the Traveling Wilburys would neither travel nor perform together a single time on a concert stage.

In addition to the Traveling Wilburys, the 1980s saw the formation of several other memorable all-star bands such as Bad English, the Damn Yankees, the Power Station and Asia. In fact, there's a long tradition of supergroups in rock history. But for every successful act like Cream, Blind Faith or Emerson, Lake & Palmer, there are dozens of promising but forgotten groups such as Oysterhead, Gogmagog and Zwan.

As one rock critic wrote, "Supergroups are almost always a disaster.... The reason supergroups are routinely tumultuous is that they're rooted in an awkward balance of egos. Where a band typically learns to blend its individual personalities while struggling toward success, the supergroup is composed of performers already accustomed to the perks and prerogatives of stardom. Where a hungry band might argue about who ate the last slice of pizza, supergroups tussle over more substantive issues. Like the spotlight." As George Harrison conceded, "Just getting some famous people together doesn't guarantee success. More often than not it's just a clash of personalities and a big ego detour."

A writer at *American Songwriter* remarked, "The effortless camaraderie amongst titans of the music world might be the thing that distinguishes the Traveling Wilburys from other supergroups." Another thing that set the Wilburys apart from other similar outfits was the strong, proven songwriting skills of every member of the group.

Wanting to avoid the classic pitfalls, Petty argued at the time: "We definitely didn't want to treat this like a supergroup. I don't even like the term all that much. But we were aware that it would be viewed as such. We look at the Wilburys as a completely other persona."

Surprisingly, in the wake of the Wilburys' success, other rock artists did not pursue similar projects. Who knows what a group consisting of Bono, Paul McCartney, Bruce Springsteen, Billy Joel and Jerry Lee Lewis would have sounded like? But one of Harrison's former bandmates did go the supergroup route, albeit in a novel manner, with a continuous shuffling of its members. It was no coincidence that Ringo Starr launched his annual All-Starr Band revue in 1989, which has featured everyone from Joe Walsh and Billy Preston to Randy Bachman and Stevie Nicks. Even Jeff Lynne performed at one show.

In addition to chronicling the history of the Traveling Wilburys, this book will examine how the various members of the group interacted with one another, how they influenced each other's personal lives and professional careers, and how they contributed to each other's musical legacies. Portions of this book originally appeared in the biography, *Tom Petty: An American Rock and Roll Story*.

▶ CHAPTER 1
DYLAN AND PETTY

As the often repeated story goes, the Traveling Wilburys came together when George Harrison needed to quickly record a new track for the B-side of an upcoming European single from his comeback album, *Cloud Nine*. But the path to recording the song, which featured four of his musical colleagues, was not a matter of pure chance.

Just five years earlier, most of the group's members barely knew each other. But after a string of fortuitous encounters, a few of them became fast friends and close confidants. While some of the men had known each other for just a short period, others had crossed paths on many occasions and influenced each other in numerous ways.

Bob Dylan and George Harrison had already established a close, two-decade-old friendship. Beginning in the mid-1960s, they had nurtured a deep respect for each other and had collaborated on various projects.

The origins of the Traveling Wilburys can be traced to a

number of key events. One of these occurred on a very hot July day in 1985. In between songs at an outdoor charity concert, Bob Dylan uttered a seemingly innocent statement, which deeply offended the promoter of the event. But the heartfelt comment directly led to the creation of another charity concert and would put Dylan together on a stage with a future member of the Wilburys – Tom Petty.

Dylan made his statement in front of a worldwide audience of nearly two-billion viewers while onstage at the Live Aid concert in Philadelphia. Organized by Bob Geldof of the Boomtown Rats, Live Aid was staged in two cities on the same day.

Tom Petty and the Heartbreakers were in the middle of a tour and flew in from Florida to perform at JFK Stadium. Neither Dylan nor Petty were strangers to the charity concert circuit and three years earlier, both artists performed at the Peace Sunday fundraiser at the Rose Bowl in Pasadena. At the time, the two men barely knew each other and were distant acquaintances.

Live Aid nearly featured a third future Traveling Wilbury. George Harrison declined the opportunity to join Paul McCartney for a duet of the Beatles classic "Let It Be," and angrily remarked, "Paul didn't ask me to sing on [the song] ten years ago, why does he want me now?"

Dylan, the headliner at the Philadelphia portion of Live Aid, would soon play an important role in Petty's career. Geldof recalled the difficulty in bringing aboard the legendary folk-rocker: "I had called Dylan through everybody: personal friends, lawyers, [his] record company. He never said no, he'd also never said yes. Usually he spends the summer with his children on the West Coast, but we needed the person who articulated the conscience of an earlier generation." A week before the concert, Dylan's participation was confirmed by his manager.

Introduced by a grinning Jack Nicholson, Dylan was the final act of the landmark event. Backed by Keith Richards and Ronnie Wood, Dylan performed three songs including "Blowin' In The Wind." But Dylan would soon create a storm of controversy during an unscripted moment between songs when he suggested that a small portion of the funds should go to struggling American farmers: "I'd like to say I hope some of the money that's raised for the people in Africa, maybe they could take a little bit of it – maybe one or two million, maybe – and use it to pay the mortgages on some of the farms.... the farmers here owe to the banks." Upon hearing the short monologue, Bob Geldof was incensed. He later called Dylan's actions, "crass, stupid and nationalistic." (Years later, Dylan would skip a similar event organized by Geldof in 2005 called Live 8.)

But Dylan's public plea to help American farmers directly led to the creation of another fundraising concert. Just one month after Dylan made his comment at Live Aid, singer Willie Nelson – who spent several summers picking cotton and corn during his youth in Texas – began planning the inaugural Farm Aid benefit concert. Naturally, Nelson asked Dylan to be a part of the event. Taking place a mere ten weeks after the Live Aid concert, Farm Aid was staged on September 22 at the University of Illinois Memorial Stadium in the town of Champaign.

When Dylan mentioned to Neil Young, one of the performers and organizers of Farm Aid, that he wanted an established rock act as his backing band, Young suggested Tom Petty and the Heartbreakers, who were also on the bill. Dylan had previously worked with most of the Heartbreakers: Benmont Tench had performed on Dylan's 1981 album *Shot Of Love*, and Tench was joined by Mike Campbell and Howie Epstein on 1985's *Empire Burlesque*. Petty had first met "the Voice of a Generation" in June 1978 when he was given free tickets to a Dylan concert at the Universal Amphitheater in Los Angeles. After the show, Petty was invited backstage to meet Dylan.

To prepare for Farm Aid, Dylan joined the Heartbreakers for some practice sessions at the Universal Sound Stage in Los Angeles. Petty recalled: "We spent a week rehearsing... and we would play a lot every night. Hours and hours and hours. We did Hank Williams songs, Motown songs.... We even played 'Louie Louie' one night. And 'Then He Kissed Me,' the old Crystals song." On the final day of rehearsals, a camera crew from the ABC news program, *20/20*, filmed Dylan for a profile of the artist.

But despite the many hours spent practicing, Dylan and Petty were perfectionists who decided to visit the site of the event on the night before their scheduled performance. As Buddy Lee, the promoter of the first Farm Aid concert, recalled: "There was nobody in the stadium, just a very small crew.... Everybody else had gone to bed, but we were doing the final checks before calling it a night. Bob Dylan had requested a sound check. We weren't giving sound checks to anybody because we were still painting the stage at the time – that's how quick everything had to fall into place. But he wanted a sound check. The only time he could have a sound check was at midnight. He came in a van with Tom Petty.... Dylan, Petty, and the Heartbreakers played their whole set to about ten of us. That was a magic moment." Dylan and Petty would run through several songs, closing with a rendition of Chris Kenner's "I Like It Like That."

On the following morning, Farm Aid opened at 10 AM with 78,000 spectators packed into the massive 62-year-old football stadium. The 14-hour musical marathon aired on the Nashville Network, which billed the event as "A Concert for America." After Tom Petty and the Heartbreakers performed four songs – including a spirited rendition of the Animals' classic "Don't Bring Me Down" – Dylan joined the group for an additional set, which was highlighted by the protest song, "Maggie's Farm." The Dylan/Petty collaboration was well received by the large crowd. Petty recalled: "When we went to the gig, we only did twenty minutes, so everyone was saying, 'Boy, it's a shame we can't really play for a while.'" Also on the bill at Farm Aid was another legendary rocker and future Wilbury, Roy Orbison. Dressed in black and wearing his trademark, dark Ray-Ban sunglasses, Orbison – who was called "the greatest singer in the world" by Elvis Presley – gave a convincing performance. Playing his classics such as "Crying," "Mean Woman Blues" and the best-received song of his short set, "Oh, Pretty Woman," Orbison seemed genuinely happy to be on the stage.

With the Farm Aid concert raising $9 million for American family-owned farms, the organizers decided to stage the event on an annual basis. Bob Dylan would later comment: "Live Aid and Farm Aid are fantastic things, but then musicians have always done things like that. When people want a benefit, you don't see them calling dancers or architects or lawyers or even politicians – the power of music is that it has always drawn people together."

Two years later, Dylan would perform at another all-star charity event, the making of the "We Are The World" video. That would place Dylan as the only performer who participated in all three major, musical charity events of the 1980s.

▶ CHAPTER 2
DYLAN & THE HEARTBREAKERS

When Tom Petty received a telephone call in July 1985, asking if he would like to team with Bob Dylan for a five-week tour, an excited Petty replied, "Are you kidding? Put me down. Send me the itinerary!" Suddenly, Petty found himself preparing to tour with a musical icon. He admitted, "I was a little nervous at first. I didn't know Bob very well, and he's a hard person to know. He turned out to be a good friend. Some of our best times were on the plane rides."

In December, Bob Dylan joined Tom Petty and the Heartbreakers for a few weeks of rehearsals. Bass player Howie Epstein described the unorthodox daily sessions: "[Dylan would say], 'here's the song, here's the chords, let's do it.' There are no arrangements, we just play."

Dubbed the True Confessions Tour, the Far East jaunt began in New Zealand and continued with fourteen shows across Australia and then four in Japan. The tour's first date in Wellington, New Zealand, was nearly cancelled by angry city officials "after the under-rehearsed band whipped up the ire of local residents by turning an outdoor sound check at Athletic Park into a lengthy, full-volume practice session. Tempers eventually calmed, however, and the show went on."

But the concert did not go smoothly. *Rolling Stone* reported: "According to some reviews, the tour got off to a shaky start in New Zealand, where the opening-night audiences responded more fervently to Petty's set than Dylan's. But within a few shows, Dylan was storming into such songs as 'Clean Cut Kid,' 'Positively 4th Street,' 'Rainy Day Women' and 'Like A Rolling Stone,' often facing off with Campbell and Petty in fierce three-way guitar exchanges and launching suddenly into songs that nobody had rehearsed, and that some band members hardly knew." While in New Zealand, Dylan secretly became a father for the sixth time, with a woman he would marry – also in secret – later that year.

During the tour, Dylan and Petty were occasionally joined by guitarist Mark Knopfler of Dire Straits. Additionally, Petty invited Stevie Nicks to join the Australian leg of the tour as a surprise guest. Nicks later recalled, "I got to sing 'Knockin' On Heaven's Door' with Bob and Tom! I'll never forget... walking out to perform and having Bob Dylan turn and do a little bow. It made everything all right – all the pain, all the trouble, all the hassles that come along with this kind of a life in rock and roll. They all went away that moment."

While in Australia, Petty and Dylan recorded the politically-incendiary blues-rock track, "Band Of The Hand," for the film of the same name, which was directed by Paul Michael Glaser. Produced by Petty, the song featured Dylan on lead vocal with

Stevie Nicks providing the harmonies. Despite the massive amount of media coverage surrounding the Dylan/Petty tour, the song was not embraced by radio.

Meanwhile, a documentary culled from two concerts in Sydney was broadcast on HBO and later issued on home video as *Hard To Handle*. The concert film captured Dylan and Petty hitting their stride, particularly on the track, "Knockin' On Heaven's Door." But for whatever reasons, the film's producers focused on Dylan and nearly ignored Petty's contributions. During this period, Petty was continually quizzed about his touring partner: "Everyone's always saying to me, 'What's Bob Dylan like?' It's funny, but people still attach a lot of mystery to Bob... I think they figure that, since we've spent time around him, we can *explain* him, as if he's somebody who needs to be explained. I mean, Dylan's just a guy like anybody else – except he's a guy who has something to say. And he has a personality that makes it his own. There's not many people that can walk into a room of 20,000, stare at them and get their attention."

During the tour, Petty was also very careful not to mimic Dylan's vocal style: "As a matter of fact, I try to avoid singing like Dylan, just because I don't want to seem like I'm imitating him. I have been conscious of that." Heartbreakers guitarist Mike Campbell would later say of Dylan and the tour: "It was kind of like anarchy in a sense, good anarchy. His approach to things was so different. With our band, we have a showbiz ethic: You try to give the people what they want, you try to get them to cheer, you try to win the game. Bob is like 'I'll do what I want and they'll come to me. I don't need to entertain them.'"

In April, Petty and Dylan announced an extension of their tour, with 22 U.S. dates scheduled for the months of June and July. One music critic observed at the time: "It's a sure bet that Petty and the Heartbreakers, far more of a star attraction on the concert circuit these days, have helped business."

Taking a three-month break from the road, Tom Petty and the Heartbreakers entered a recording studio to back Dylan on his 24th studio album, *Knocked Out Loaded*. The group was joined on the sessions by a litany of guest musicians including Al Kooper, Dave Stewart, Ronnie Wood, and T Bone Burnett. Not one of Dylan's better albums, the project included a composition Petty composed with Dylan, "Got My Mind Made Up," which Dylan historian Howard Sounes called "one of the most forgettable songs of Bob's career." In exchange for helping to produce the album, Petty was given a work of art – a Dylan self-portrait. The painting later found a home on the wall of Petty's basement recording studio.

Going back on the road, the Dylan/Petty rock ensemble began the U.S. portion of the tour on June 9, with a stop at the San Diego Sports Arena. A reviewer said of the performance: "If the audience wanted a chance to hear more of Petty's material, he seemed to revel in not having to be in the spotlight. He joined Dylan at the microphone to share vocals several times, but, more often, he simply looked like an artist who was thrilled to be playing with one of his major influences."

Beginning with a performance in Minneapolis on June 26, Dylan and Petty teamed with the legendary Grateful Dead for a handful of stadium shows. Dylan and Grateful Dead leader Jerry Garcia were longtime friends and decided to schedule five summer concerts. Admission to these shows was a mere $20.

In August 1986, Dylan turned to acting in the big screen drama, *Hearts Of Fire*. In the film, he portrayed a reclusive, Harley-riding rock singer whose career was in decline. The film was not a box office success.

▶ CHAPTER 3
THE CLOSE OF THE DYLAN / PETTY TOUR

In late August 1987, Tom Petty and the Heartbreakers reunited with Bob Dylan and began rehearsing for the next leg of their extended tour. At one point, Dylan and Heartbreakers drummer Stan Lynch missed a night of practice so they could attend a concert in Los Angeles. As Lynch recalled, "I took Dylan to see Sammy [Davis, Jr.] and Frank [Sinatra] at the Greek Theater.... That's a true story. The first week of rehearsals for the Dylan tour, Dylan hadn't spoken to us all week. We were all playing and I said, 'Look, I gotta bug out early tonight.' And they go, 'Lynch, what's your crisis?' I go, 'I got tickets for Sammy and Frank at the Greek.' The whole band covers their eyes going, 'Oh geez, I can't believe he really said that.' And Dylan looked up at me in all seriousness and said, 'Sammy and Frank? I love those guys.' So Dylan and I went to the Greek.... I don't mind saying I was a little starstruck by the whole concept that I came from Gainesville to L.A., and now I'm sitting with Bob Dylan watching Sammy Davis and Frank Sinatra."

The Temples in Flames tour began with two dates in Israel. Afterwards, a member of Dylan's entourage observed: "For the next few concerts, we kept our tours separate from Tom's, despite playing the same shows. We didn't move at the same time, we didn't use the same equipment; we didn't use the same boats or planes to travel. It was very odd to me; the relationship didn't exist behind the curtain like it did onstage. Onstage they would sing a couple songs a night together and from the audience's point of view they were friends, but their relationship was far from developing to what it is today."

Dylan and Petty then headed to Europe for nearly thirty shows over the next six weeks. Dylan recalled, "In these first four shows I sang eighty different songs, never repeating one, just to see if I could do it. It seemed easy." Near the end of the highly successful tour, the rock and roll troupe performed for three nights at the National Exhibition Centre in Birmingham, England. Present at the shows were George Harrison and Jeff Lynne. Backstage, Lynne and Petty would meet for the very first time. It was here that the seeds for a future collaboration were planted.

The tour's final dates – four shows at the Wembley Arena in London – took place in mid-October. Backstage, much of Britain's rock's royalty had assembled to watch Dylan and Petty. According to one observer: "There are a hundred requests for backstage passes, including some for Mark Knopfler, George Harrison, Julian Lennon, Keith Richards, and Randy Jackson."

Also backstage, Mike Campbell experienced a heart-stopping moment when he stood, face to face, with a former

Beatle: "We were pretty worn out. George and Jeff came by backstage. George walked up to me and I said 'hi,' and he did one of those things where instead of shaking hands he took my hand in both of his hands, looked me right in the eye and goes, 'Bless you.' I remember thinking, 'Wow, this is a heavy cat.' It was a sweet gesture and I felt a connection."

Harrison would subsequently join Dylan and Petty onstage for an encore performance of "Rainy Day Women #12 & 35." For a brief moment, four-fifths of the soon-to-be-formed Traveling Wilburys were within arm's reach of each other.

The toured finally ended on October 17, 1987. Although he deeply cherished his two-year collaboration with Dylan, Petty knew the tour had to come to an end. Petty needed to rebuild his home – which had been torched by an arsonist earlier in the year – and tend to his wife and young daughters. Petty came to a realization after the London concert: "I just thought, okay, it's time to get off this bus now and get back to being us. I think he thought we could do both, but we couldn't [because] it was wearing me out." Though disappointed by the news, Dylan – himself a strong family man who fawned over his children – did not try to change Petty's mind.

Touring with Dylan had been a psychologically-cleansing experience for Petty: "By the time we got out on the tour with him in Australia, I just felt really free for some reason. Everything was clear again. I was so busy focusing on playing well that I forgot about all my problems. I was enjoying music again. I realized that I was worrying too much about pleasing other people or being accepted."

Although the tour had been a career high for Petty, the same could not be said for Dylan. He later revealed in his autobiography: "I'd been on an eighteen month tour with Tom Petty and the Heartbreakers.... I had no connection to any kind of inspiration. Whatever was there to begin with had vanished and shrunk. Tom was at the top of his game and I was at the bottom of mine. I couldn't overcome the odds. Everything was smashed. I didn't have the skill to touch their raw nerves. Couldn't penetrate the surfaces. It wasn't my moment of history anymore. There was a hollow singing in my heart and I couldn't wait to retire and fold the tent." Notable British deejay John Peel was far more brutal about one of the final shows: "Being an enigma at 20 is fun, being an enigma at 30 shows a lack of imagination, and being an enigma at Dylan's age is just plain daft – from the moment the living legend took to the stage, it was evident that here was business he wanted accomplished with the minimum of effort."

At the end of the tour, Dylan was invited to spend some time at the home of George Harrison. Afterwards, Dylan took a cruise on the Caribbean before heading back home.

A few months later, in January 1988, two future members of the Traveling Wilburys were inducted into the Rock and Roll Hall of Fame, Bob Dylan and George Harrison (as a member of the Beatles). Mick Jagger inducted his one-time rivals, jokingly calling the group a "four-headed monster." Jagger opened his speech with the comment: "When I got here tonight, I saw George and he said, 'You're not going to say anything bad about me, are you?'"

John Fogerty recalled seeing Harrison at the induction ceremony: "He was seated at a table, and there was a buzz of people around him. He'd had so much success but it was happening all over again – this time in the MTV age, with videos and everything. It was thrilling. As a fan, you just love to watch your heroes ride the shooting star again. I walked up to him and said, 'How's it feel to be the hottest guy in show business?' And he said, 'It's a bloody nuisance!'"

When Harrison took the stage to acknowledge the induction of the Beatles, he stated: "I don't have to say much because I'm the quiet Beatle. It is unfortunate Paul's not here because he's the one who had the speech in his pocket."

McCartney had boycotted the ceremony due to pending legal issues with his former bandmates. He released the statement: "After 20 years, the Beatles still have some business differences, which I had hoped would have been settled by now. Unfortunately, they haven't been, so I would feel like a complete hypocrite waving and smiling with them at a fake reunion."

Bruce Springsteen, who had previously inducted Roy Orbison in 1987, was back to induct Bob Dylan. In his address, Springsteen said: "The first time I heard Bob Dylan, I was in the car with my mother listening to WMCA, and on came that snare shot that sounded like somebody'd kicked open the door to your mind... The way that Elvis freed your body, Dylan freed your mind."

Taking the stage, Dylan spoke for a mere one minute and sixteen seconds, during which time he thanked Springsteen, the board at the Rock Hall, Little Richard and Alan Lomax, and then said "hi" to Muhammad Ali. He closed his comments with a bit of Dylanesque wit: "Peace, love and harmony is greatly important, indeed, but so is forgiveness and we gotta have that, too."

Dylan later led a disjointed rendition of his classic, "Like A Rolling Stone." Behind him were several guitarists, including Jeff Lynne and George Harrison. Dylan then shared a microphone with Harrison for an all-star rendition of the Dylan gem made by popular by Jimi Hendrix, "All Along The Watchtower." Joining the pair on stage were Springsteen, Fogerty, Jagger, Little Richard and many others.

▶ CHAPTER 4
CROSSING PATHS: GEORGE, TOM & ROY

Tom Petty had first crossed paths with George Harrison a few years before forming the Heartbreakers: "I first met him in 1974 when I came out to Los Angeles. I hadn't been out here very long. I was working at Leon Russell's [home studio], and there were a few nights [of] sessions with George and Ringo. It's a scary thing meeting Beatles, but George was so nice to me and included me in everything."

Then during the European leg of the tour with Bob Dylan, Petty had a few opportunities to speak with Harrison: "I reminded him that we'd met, and there was some kind of weird click. It felt like we had known each other all our lives, and in a very personal way."

In fact, Petty had been a huge Beatles fan since age 13, ever since he watched them make their triumphant U.S. television debut on February 9, 1964. Appearing on *The Ed Sullivan Show*, the Beatles would soon reshape the American musical landscape. Exactly two months later, the Beatles would hold down all five of the top-five positions on *Billboard* magazine's Hot 100 singles chart.

Beatlemania had arrived and young Tom was in the grip of the movement's seismic revolution. "They came out and just flattened me. To hear them on the radio was amazing enough, but to finally see them play, it was electrifying. They did those three songs at the top of the show and then you had to wait till the end for them to come back on. It felt like an eternity, watching these comedy skits and, like, guys spinning plates – and remember, this is the biggest show on TV, but to us kids, we wanted the Beatles, so to have to watch a guy spinning plates, it was total torture. Plus, the girls screaming – I never seen or heard anything like that in my life. Girls were going insane, crying and waving. You just knew the TV studio was being turned upside down," Petty recalled. Petty soon bought a Lennon and McCartney songbook and taught himself how to play the group's early hits.

Upon Tom Petty's return to California after the completion of the Dylan/Petty tour, destiny seemed to take over. Petty recalled what happened: "I went back to L.A., and almost by fate I went into a restaurant, spur of the moment. I hadn't planned to go, and the waiter came over and said, 'Oh, your friend is in the next room, he wants to see you.' I didn't know who he meant. I walked in, and it was George. He said, 'God, it's so weird, I was just asking Jeff Lynne for your number.' He said, 'Where are you going?' I said, 'I'm just going home.' He said, 'Do you mind if I go with you?' He came to my house and stayed for days. George came to L.A. fairly often, and I went to England and visited him a lot." Within a few months, Petty's daughter Adria and George's son Dhani also became very close friends.

Petty would soon find himself in an unimaginable position as a member of a group which included one of his early musical idols. Petty recounted, "We weren't even thinking about being in a band together, but we loved having a few beers and just talking, just visiting. Kind of like when you see people and feel like you've known them for a long time. That's how I related to George and Jeff. Then I came home and I was at a red light Thanksgiving Day, going to buy some baseball gloves, 'cause I wanted to play baseball real bad and the only place open was Thrifty Drugs. Now George had given me his *Cloud Nine* album just before it was released. I loved it and I'd been playing it all day before I went to get these mitts. So when I get to this light, and there's Jeff, the next car over.... He was going to produce Brian Wilson at the time. And he said, 'Do you want to come to the studio with me?' I said, 'Nah, I'm going to play baseball.' But we agreed to stay in touch and it turned out he lived in my neighborhood, just up the street." According to Petty, "I told him where I lived and he came over for the next six months."

Meanwhile, George Harrison and Roy Orbison had first met in May 1963, when the Beatles were scheduled as the *opening*

act for Orbison during a three-week tour across Britain. What Orbison did not know at the time, the Fab Four's second British single, "Please Please Me," had been written by John Lennon in an attempt to emulate Orbison. And according to one of Orbison's sons, Lennon and McCartney had based "Love Me Do" on the Orbison song, "Candy Man."

Early in the tour, Lennon and Beatles manager Brian Epstein demanded a reversal in the billing – with the Beatles closing the shows as the headliners. Orbison graciously consented. As Orbison remembered: "I agreed because I was singing ballads and they were singing songs like 'Twist And Shout,' so it all made sense. Anyway, I was making four or five times as much money as they were, so I gave them a break. As you can see, it was the right move."

On the opening night of the tour at the Adelphi Theatre near London, Orbison was a smash hit with the boisterous audience, which kept screaming for additional encores. But "when Roy started to go back on stage, Lennon and McCartney could restrain themselves no longer, grabbing him by the arms and refusing to let him take his curtain call. Roy struggled, but John said, '*Yankee, go home!*'" Ringo Starr would later admit, "Roy Orbison was the only act that the Beatles didn't want to follow."

Eventually, Orbison and the members of the Beatles would establish a warm relationship. With both Orbison and Harrison regularly sleeping in late and missing their ride to the next stop on the tour, the two men shared a number of amicable conversations during long car or train rides.

While many American pop and rock acts were unable to

survive the arrival of the British Invasion, Orbison continued to thrive. In 1964, he even managed to top the British charts twice, with the singles "Oh, Pretty Woman" and "It's Over."

Back in the U.S., Orbison also became friends with Bob Dylan during this period. Dylan was a fan of Orbison's music, and once offered the praise: "His songs had songs within songs.... There wasn't anything else on the radio like him." Before he was a folkie, Dylan had been a fan of early rock and roll. In 1959, Dylan briefly joined a band led by Bobby Vee. And in his high school yearbook, Dylan wrote that his life's ambition was "to join the band of Little Richard."

In 1963, a young Dylan would ask Orbison to record the track, "Don't Think Twice, It's All Right." Rejecting the Dylan composition, Orbison would later regret his decision.

Later, when the Beatles made their triumphant first trek across America in 1964, they asked Orbison to join the tour as an opening act. Unfortunately, he had prior commitments. (The following year when Orbison was booked as the opening act for the Rolling Stones, he managed to steal some of the British band's thunder, which did not please Mick Jagger.) The Beatles and Orbison would perform on the same bill just one more time. On May 1, 1966, they both appeared at *The New Musical Express* Annual Poll-Winners All-Star Concert at the Empire Pool in London.

Meanwhile, across the Atlantic on August 28, 1964, several months after Beatlemania had hit the U.S. shores, 21-year-old George Harrison first met Bob Dylan, who was just two years his senior. With the Beatles preparing for a concert in New York City, Dylan visited the group at the 32-story Delmonico

Hotel. Although John Lennon was absorbed with the young American folk singer and had invited him to the group's hotel room, the other members of the Beatles also treated Dylan with the utmost admiration and were in awe of his second album, *The Freewheelin' Bob Dylan*. A hipster who was wise to the ways of the world, Dylan rolled a joint for each member of the group during his visit. (Although the members of the Fab Four had experienced their own share of vice while playing in the seedy nightclubs of Hamburg, they had only briefly experimented with marijuana in the past.)

As innovators and rule breakers, both Dylan and the Beatles had much to learn from each other. Dylan demonstrated that rock and roll would embrace intelligent lyrics and biting social commentary. At the same time, he also proved that having a commanding, trained voice was not as important as possessing strong songwriting skills. Meanwhile, the Beatles also ignored the established rules of rock and roll, and introduced various innovations to the genre, including classical instruments, concept albums, studio gadgetry – such as spliced audio loops, intentional feedback and back masking – and the printing of song lyrics on album covers.

Later, in an attempt to keep up with the shifting tastes in popular music, Dylan went electric in 1965. But when folk purists viciously attacked Dylan, Harrison publically came to his defense: "The people who walked out [of his concerts] must have been idiots.... It was all still pure Dylan, and he has to find out his own directions. If he felt he wanted electrification, that's the way he had to do it. Who's laying down the rules?" Also that year, Dylan made an offer to the Fab Four at a hotel in

London: "Hey – I got an idea. Why don't you guys write a song and I'll record it, and I'll write a song for you to do? But I'll write a real good song, so don't write me no 'Please Please Me' kind of thing." Neither Dylan nor the Beatles ever got around to writing the songs.

Then, four years after their initial meeting, Harrison and Dylan spent several days together during the Thanksgiving holiday at Dylan's home in Woodstock, New York. Harrison brought along his wife, Pattie, and Dylan was with his wife, Sara, and their children. It was during this time that Dylan and Harrison decided to collaborate on some songs. Their first creation, "I'd Have You Anytime," later appeared on Harrison's first post-Beatles solo album. As author Marc Shapiro observed in *All Things Must Pass: The Life of George Harrison*: "George, in his late twenties and showing a marked sense of maturity when it came to music, went back to the United States for a visit with Bob Dylan. During this visit, all barriers came down and the two musicians were able to deal with each other as people. During this visit, Dylan was generous and forthcoming in inviting George into his latest musical vision, sitting together for hours, swapping lyrics, chords and ideas. George came away from his visit with Bob Dylan renewed, inspired and anxious to make new and personal music away from the glare of the Beatles spotlight." In the wake of his sojourn with Dylan, Harrison composed "Old Brown Shoe," which the Beatles would record in 1969.

Harrison soon became quite fond of Dylan. As drummer Jim Keltner recalled, "He was Bob's biggest fan. He could quote the lyrics to practically any Dylan song you came up with."

Also in 1969, Dylan traveled to Nashville to record his seminal album, *Nashville Skyline*. Wanting Orbison to perform on the project, Dylan made a surprise visit to Orbison's home. But while Orbison's wife was at home to take Dylan's message, "The Big O" was touring across Canada at the time.

The following year, Harrison visited Dylan during the sessions for the album, *Self Portrait*. In the studio, the two men were joined by Russ Kunkel on drums and Charlie Daniels on bass guitar. Daniels later recalled: "It was a day I'll never forget. It wasn't Bob Dylan and George Harrison. It was four guys in the studio making music. Anything you threw at [Bob], he could sing... It was such a nice thing, such a great day, hour after hour." Unfortunately, none of the tracks recorded that day appeared on the album.

Also in 1970, Harrison recorded the Dylan original "If Not For You," which later became the debut hit for Aussie singer Olivia Newton-John. Then in 1971, Dylan performed at Harrison's high-profile charity benefit, the Concert for Bangladesh. Dylan's appearance at the event was not certain and Harrison was genuinely surprised to see the reclusive folk-rock legend when he walked onto the stage.

Meanwhile, while Orbison's popularity had dramatically cooled in the U.S. during the late-1960s, he continued to remain a strong draw in the U.K. In fact, he managed to headline the prestigious Royal Albert Hall in 1972.

▶ CHAPTER 5
THE BEATLES SPAWN ELO

In 1970, just as the Beatles were breaking up, a British rock band – the Move – hired 22-year-old Jeff Lynne as a pianist and second guitarist. The group, which was inspired by the Beatles' complex orchestral sound, would eventually evolve into the Electric Light Orchestra, one of the very few rock groups that toured with its own classical string section. On stage, the Move frequently performed the Beatles song "She's A Woman."

Before his involvement in the Move and ELO, Lynne was a member of another band, the Idle Race. While recording the group's debut album in 1968, Lynne met George Harrison for the first time. Harrison had invited Lynne to a Beatles session at Abbey Road Studios. Meeting the Fab Four and watching producer George Martin at work, Lynne was in complete awe. Lynne later recalled, "I went into the studio there at Abbey Road. Walked into the room where John (Lennon) and George (Harrison) were. They were watching through the window as George Martin conducted the strings on 'Glass Onion.' That was such a privilege to see that. Like seeing history itself." An overwhelmed Lynne was unable to sleep for days after the encounter. Ironically, twenty years later, Lynne and one of the Beatles would be members of the same band.

In time, Lynne would consciously attempt to emulate the Beatles' musical style. While numerous music writers have accused him of directly copying the Fab Four, Lynne took the criticism as a compliment. The influence of the Beatles was blatantly apparent on a number of ELO tracks in the 1970s. Songs like "Telephone Line," "Can't Get It Out Of My Head," "Strange Magic," "Livin' Thing" and "Do Ya" seemed right at home on latter Beatles projects such as *Abbey Road* or *The White Album*. Paul McCartney has acknowledged that much of ELO's output is comparable to what the Beatles accomplished during their *Sgt. Pepper* period. In fact, ELO's 1979 hit "Don't Bring Me Down" was rumored at the time to be a long-lost Beatles song. But unlike the Beatles who were guided in the recording studio by the masterful producer George Martin, Lynne was not aided by a musical mentor and was the producer or co-producer of ELO's entire output.

During a 1974 radio interview on WNEW in New York City, John Lennon proclaimed his respect for ELO: "I call them 'Son of Beatles,' although they're doing things that we never did, obviously. But I remember the statement they made when they first formed was to carry on where the Beatles left off with 'Walrus' – and they certainly did." Lennon would identify "Showdown" as his favorite ELO song.

Starting with the 1972 British top-10 single "10538 Overture," ELO was very successful on both sides of the

Atlantic. As one music critic proclaimed: "Between 1972 and 1986, ELO put more singles in the combined U.S. and U.K. Top 40 charts than any other band in the world. Somebody had to be buying them."

Lynne would meet a second Wilbury for the first time in 1978 during the middle of ELO's *Out Of The Blue* tour at a concert stop in Japan. Lynne recalled: "I first met Bob [Dylan] when I played Budokan in Tokyo. I looked over and he was sitting on a monitor, watching me. I thought, 'Oh, shit. I'd have done it better if I'd known he was watching.' Anyway, after the gig, I was signing autographs for a line of about 20 people. I said to this polite Japanese girl, 'Do you mind if I just take a page out of your notebook?' So I took the page and her pen and got into the [line] to get Bob Dylan's autograph." (Dylan was at Budakon to perform three shows that same week.)

By 1986, ELO went on a break and Lynne had the opportunity to indulge in other interests. But the planned hiatus soon turned into a permanent separation. While Lynne's former bandmates attempted to resurrect their own version of ELO, it wasn't until 2014 that a group calling itself Jeff Lynne's ELO returned to the stage.

During the 1980s, George Harrison would record only sporadically. It was the brutal murder of John Lennon in December 1980 that further fueled Harrison's desire to escape the limelight. He also turned his back on his career, and spent most of his time at his large estate, where he installed fences and implemented other security measures to protect himself from intruders.

In tribute to his fallen bandmate, Harrison recorded the track, "All Those Years Ago." He had originally written the song for Ringo Starr's album, *Stop And Smell The Roses*, but took it back and changed the lyrics to focus on Lennon. Recorded in May 1981, it was the first track in 11 years to feature the team of Harrison, Starr and Paul McCartney. The song was included on Harrison's ninth studio release, *Somewhere In England*. The track was the only hit from the album, which Warner Brothers was reluctant to release. A second single, "Teardrops," failed to reach *Billboard's* Hot 100.

A follow up album, 1982's *Gone Troppo*, fared even worse and was ignored by radio. Over the next five years, Harrison had effectively retired from his solo career as he preferred to be a guest artist who performed on an occasional track.

In 1987, Harrison was a musical guest at the Prince's Trust concert, which was staged at Wembley Arena in London. He performed just two songs, "While My Guitar Gently Weeps" and "Here Comes The Sun."

Also that year, Harrison joined John Fogerty and future bandmate Bob Dylan for an unplanned, two-hour concert with bluesman Taj Mahal at the relatively tiny Palomino Club in Los Angeles. Harrison had been invited to the club by Dylan. That night, Harrison performed Dylan's "Watching The River Flow," while employing a Dylanesque vocal delivery. Mahal's guitarist that night, Jesse Ed Davis, had played the guitar on Dylan's original 1971 recording. Harrison and Dylan also teamed up for a duet of the rock classic, "Peggy Sue."

✦ ✧ ✦ ✧ ✦

Meanwhile, Harrison eventually decided to record another solo album. After a long career, Harrison was experiencing some minor hearing problems and felt he needed an outside producer. He eventually hired Jeff Lynne. Although Lynne had met the former Beatle on several occasions, the two men were not friends at the time and their collaboration came by chance. They had last met while sharing a bill at a 1986 charity concert in Lynne's hometown of Birmingham, England. (While Lynne and his band, ELO, would perform more than a dozen songs, Harrison played only one track – "Johnny B. Goode.")

Later, while recording in Los Angeles, Lynne was approached by fellow British rocker Dave Edmunds. Lynne was asked by Edmunds to write a song and also help with the sessions.

After the track was completed and the two men celebrated with a fancy dinner, they exchanged goodbyes. But as Edmunds was walking away, he suddenly turned around and mentioned that George Harrison had called and wondered if Lynne would be interested in collaborating on an album. Harrison was particularly fond of the ELO hit track, "Telephone Line," and had belatedly become a fan of the group in the 1980s. Lynne later recounted: "If I could've picked one guy I wanted to work with, it would have been George. I was stunned, really."

According to recording engineer Richard Dodd, Lynne was not Harrison's first pick to produce the album. Dodd recalled: "George said, 'I'm thinking about doing a solo album. Would you like to be the engineer?' It didn't take me long to say yes.

Then he said, 'I've got an American producer and we'll see how it goes.'" After recording three tracks with the unnamed producer, Harrison did not like the sound of the songs. Instead of firing the producer, Harrison simply did not invite him back for more sessions.

John Van Der Kiste, Lynne's biographer, wrote: "Jeff was accordingly invited to meet George at his house, Friar Park, Henley-on-Thames. George took him for a spin in the boat around the lake in his garden, and they discussed collaborating. They hit it off immediately, and according to George, 'drank red wine together for a year and a half.' It was the start of a close friendship which led to them working together on and off on a regular basis until George's untimely death. When asked if he wanted to come to the Grand Prix in Australia, Jeff nodded eagerly. 'Meet me in Hawaii in two weeks.' Jeff accordingly kept the rendevous in October 1986, they flew to Adelaide together and reached the race in a helicopter, landing in the middle of the track, getting out and meeting all the teams. Jeff was astonished by the fact that George simply knew everybody." Harrison was a huge fan of Formula One racing and had developed a friendship with driver Jackie Stewart. (Stewart was the subject of Harrison's 1979 track, "Faster.")

It was during this trip when Harrison and Lynne first collaborated. While staying on an estate, located on an island off the Australian coast, the two men initially worked on the track, "When We Was Fab."

Harrison soon realized that he had made the right choice in picking Lynne as his producer. According to Harrison biographer Simon Leng, "Lynne was the strongest personality

Harrison has used in the control room since Phil Spector, and as he was an established producer in his own right, his presence was bound to have an impact. But at the time, it was an extra pair of hands that Harrison wanted. Harrison had long bemoaned the life of the 'one-man band' recording artist that he had endured on a number of his works. The pressure of writing, playing, and then producing an album was huge; using Jeff Lynne reduced the burden on him and, crucially, provided a sounding board. Lynne was no 'yes man,' and he provided the kind of honest appraisal that was so obviously lacking on [the album] *Dark Horse*. The two other keys to Lynne's role on *Cloud Nine* were his monumental love of the Beatles and his admiration of Harrison's slide guitar sound."

Although Lynne was a seasoned producer, this was his first major project outside of ELO. At Harrison's home studio, Lynne directed a number of topnotch musicians including Ringo Starr, Gary Wright, Elton John, and Eric Clapton. Also on the sessions was drummer Jim Keltner who would later record with the Traveling Wilburys.

The formal sessions for *Cloud Nine* began in January 1987. It would be Harrison's first album in five years. The songs – seventeen in all – were completed as basic tracks by March. Biographer Simon Leng suggested that the album "and the Traveling Wilburys project that followed, would probably never have happened had Carl Perkins not persuaded Harrison to play on his 1985 *Rockabilly Session* video." The Perkins tribute had reinvigorated Harrison's desire to create new music.

Meanwhile, as the sessions progressed, Lynne and Harrison became close confidants. Living at Harrison's estate for a full six-months before recording the album, Lynne would explore the vast estate full of gardens and lakes, or play soccer with Harrison's young son, Dhani.

Lynne later recalled: "We were three-quarters of the way through *Cloud Nine*, and every night, as we were relaxing with a few drinks after mixing a big epic or whatever, George and I had the same conversation, 'We could have a group, you know?' George didn't like the idea of being a solo guy – that's what he told me. He was never comfortable with it. He wanted a group, and, of course, he could do whatever he wanted."

When the album was released in November 1987, *Cloud Nine* marked a significant comeback for Harrison. While Harrison was thrilled with the success, it was not his goal. As Tom Petty recalled, "George wasn't seeking a career. He didn't really have a manager or an agent. He was doing what he wanted. I don't think he valued rock stardom at all."

The debut single, "Got My Mind Set On You," was a remake of an obscure 1962 track by James Ray. In their early years, the Beatles would perform another song by Ray (who passed away at age 31 in 1968), "If You Gotta Make A Fool Of Somebody."

A hit on pop and rock radio, "Got My Mind Set On You" topped the charts in the U.S. and nearly did the same in the U.K. The followup release, "When We Was Fab," was a reflection of Beatlemania in the 1960s. The song's music video was directed by the team of Kevin Godley and Lol Creme, and featured scenes of Harrison wearing his classic *Sgt. Pepper* suit and Lynne playing the violin. This would be Harrison's final top-40 solo hit in the U.S.

▶ CHAPTER 6
TOM PETTY & JEFF LYNNE

After listening to George Harrison's completed album, Tom Petty was impressed with Lynne's contributions to the project. Petty had been given a demo version of the album while in London at the end of the Dylan/Petty tour.

Running into Lynne on a Los Angeles street during the first week of January 1987, Petty invited him to a backyard barbecue. Unable to attend, Lynne had previous obligations. Petty then offered a different invitation and asked if he would like to come over the next day and work on some music.

When Lynne arrived, Petty asked him for some help on a solo project. This wasn't the first time that Petty had asked for Lynne's assistance. A decade earlier when the debut Heartbreakers album captured the attention of the American public, the group was caught by surprise and desperately wanted to return to the studio as quickly as possible. Out of necessity, Petty and the Heartbreakers approached the sessions for their second album with a sense of urgency. Petty attempted to hire Lynne to produce the album, but was told, "well, he doesn't do outside projects."

This time around, Petty was a major star and ELO had essentially broken up the previous year. Although Lynne was in a rush to return to England, he was persuaded to remain in Los Angeles for another week. Petty recounted: "We started playing around at home. I'd written this song called 'Yer So Bad.' I played it for Jeff; he suggested a couple of chords, which made it so much better. I couldn't believe how good it sounded. So we wrote another one, 'Free Fallin'.' Being immensely pleased with them, I wanted to get them on tape somehow. The only place I knew to go was [Mike Campbell's home studio]. The Heartbreakers weren't even in town, so we called up Phil Jones, this brilliant drummer we'd known for years, and went in and cut these two songs. When they were done, they were like records. They weren't demos, by any stretch of the imagination."

Thrilled with the sessions, Petty explained, "I remember coming home with those two songs on a cassette and playing them over and over, just saying, 'Wow, this is really good.' I had to talk Jeff into finishing the album with me." Although Petty was steadfast about Lynne taking over the production duties, Lynne was apprehensive about accepting the job offer. Petty recounted: "He was very nervous about overtaking the record. He didn't want it to sound like Jeff Lynne. He wanted it to sound like me. I had no qualms whatsoever with having Jeff produce me, especially after the job he did on George's *Cloud Nine*. That's an incredible sounding record. It's just so much louder and sounds more exciting than other records.

Whatever you think of ELO, you have to admit those records were very well produced."

Soon after, Petty experienced another spark of musical creativity: "While they were mixing [the two tracks], we went into a little soundproof booth at this studio and wrote 'I Won't Back Down.' By the time those [two] songs were mixed, we were sitting on another song that we went in the next day and recorded." During the sessions for "I Won't Back Down," George Harrison stopped by and provided some guitarwork and harmony vocals. (At one point in the sessions, Harrison suggested some lyrical changes, which Petty adopted.)

Those three soon-to-be rock classics were written and recorded in just three days. Petty later explained: "All the songs were written on 12-string or 6-string acoustic guitars. I wanted to experiment with the art of rhythm guitar. Jeff and I feel that acoustic guitars can be rock 'n' roll instruments, not just folk instruments."

During this period, Petty would complete most of the album's tracks. Putting aside his solo project, he was soon immersed in another musical venture.

▶ CHAPTER 7
ROY ORBISON MAKES A COMEBACK

Tom Petty recalled a conversation he had in 1988, "So [Jeff Lynne] had Roy [Orbison] over one day and wondered if I wanted to write some songs with him. I didn't really know him. That's sort of when we first got to know each other and wrote a couple songs, 'You Got It' and 'California Blue.'"

Reminiscing about Orbison, Petty later recounted: "The first time that I heard him was on the family radio. We had this Arvin electric radio and he came over the air and it was in the afternoon after a rain. I remember the moment that I heard him. I remember that he sounded very otherworldly like he came from another place. I think it was something like probably not the obvious one, it might have been 'Only The Lonely' or 'Blue Angel.' I remember the next time I heard him was when he did 'Mean Woman Blues' and that really shook me up and I then made a point to find his records and find out exactly who this was. Not long after that 'Oh, Pretty Woman' came out and everyone knew who he was. He had that incredible stage presence with the sunglasses and this jet-black hair, he didn't really have to do anything."

The sessions for Orbison's comeback album began in the fall of 1988. It was Lynne who had first contacted Orbison with the proposition of recording an album, and it was Lynne who renewed the middle-aged crooner's confidence in the studio. Additionally, Orbison and Lynne shared one unusual attribute – both men wore dark sunglasses whenever they appeared in public.

The title of the album's first single, "You Got It," had an unusual history. According to Orbison's biographer John Kruth, "Written in Christmas '87, before the sudden, unexpected emergence of the Traveling Wilburys, the song was apparently inspired when Jeff and Roy were standing around in Petty's driveway, admiring Tom's brand new Corvette. After checking out the engine, the three musicians were momentarily stumped over how to get the hood back down. When Tom finally figured it out, one of them (presumably Roy) remarked, 'You got it!'"

A reviewer for *The Chicago Tribune* would later observe that the track "is a warmly hopeful greeting written by Orbison and newfound collaborators Jeff Lynne and Tom Petty. In many ways, it's a Wilburys' sound-alike with a light, upbeat sound, and relies on Lynne's lush production (much like his work with ELO) and the trio's combined vocals to give it a polished pop edge."

With Orbison's album taking much longer than expected, Lynne had to ask for a break in the sessions in order to complete George Harrison's album.

In time, Orbison, Lynne and Petty would return to Mike

Campbell's cluttered garage studio, where most of the album was recorded.

In 1980, Roy Orbison was enjoying a comeback on various fronts. That year, he was hired as the opening act for an Eagles tour, and he won a Grammy in the category of Best Country Performance by a Duo or Group for a duet hit with Emmylou Harris, "That Lovin' You Feeling' Again." (Ironically, it was Orbison's first-ever Grammy win.) The following year, singer Don McLean reached the top-10 with a pleading rendition of the Orbison ballad, "Crying." Then in 1982, Van Halen scored a top-40 hit with a classic rock version of the Orbison gem, "Oh, Pretty Woman."

But not all was well for Orbison. In 1982, he filed a $50 million lawsuit against Wesley Rose, accusing him of fraud and mismanaging his career. Rose had managed Orbison since 1958 and was the head of the publishing company, Acuff-Rose. The lawsuit was later settled for around $3 million.

Orbison's career revival accelerated after he moved from Nashville to Southern California in 1985. His wife, Barbara, recalled: "In the mid-80s he told me he really wanted to go for it one more time. He was 48 and he wanted to be on top of the charts at 50, doing what he loved to do."

Then, in 1986, Orbison's dramatic ballad, "In Dreams," enjoyed renewed attention after it was prominently featured in director David Lynch's violent and haunting film, *Blue Velvet*. Curiously, Lynch had used the song in the film without

Orbison's authorization. At first Orbison was upset with the song's inclusion. Lynch later explained: "It *is* a beautiful song and it was written by Roy.... Those lyrics, that feel meant something to him. And it just so happened that a song in a certain situation could mean something else.... But I can see why Roy was upset." Eventually, Orbison came to appreciate the song's use in the film, especially after it brought him some additional notoriety.

The following year, Orbison was inducted into the second class of the Rock and Roll Hall of Fame. In his tribute, Bruce Springsteen told the audience at the Waldorf-Astoria Hotel in New York City: "In 1975, when I went into the studio to make *Born To Run*, I wanted to make a record with words like Bob Dylan that sounded like Phil Spector – but most of all, I wanted to sing like Roy Orbison. Now everybody knows that no one sings like Roy Orbison." Remarkably, a 20-year-old Springsteen had been the opening act for Orbison at the Nashville Music Fair in 1970, and would later perform a number of Orbison songs in concert.

In his acceptance speech, the visibly emotional Orbison remarked, "I've spent the last 30 years trying to be cool, but now I'm nervous. You sing for many reasons, and one of them is to belong. I feel that I do truly belong."

Soon after, Orbison was the guest musical artist on *Saturday Night Live*, where he performed three songs. (A decade earlier on the same program, John Belushi portrayed Orbison and sang a faithful rendition of "Oh, Pretty Woman.")

Just months later, Springsteen, Elvis Costello, Bonnie Raitt and many others joined Orbison at the star-studded tribute, *Roy*

Orbison And Friends: A Black & White Night. Staged at the Cocoanut Grove ballroom at the Ambassador Hotel in Los Angeles, the four-hour concert was intended as a television special for Cinemax.

The tribute concert soon became a fan favorite on PBS. As author Lloyd Sachs observed: "Put into rotation as a public television pledge-drive special, *A Black & White Night* took up permanent residency in the pop culture zeitgeist. With each airing, Orbison's stature was further polished."

As Orbison's youngest son, Alex, later recalled, "My mom and dad wanted a definitive 'Roy show' as far back as when they met in 1968. When the producers... of the Cinemax series sought them out to do the show, they had already tried as many as ten times to get this kind of a show together, but it was never right. They brought on T Bone Burnett as musical director, and he called the guest artists. Legend has it that several of the guest artists had gigs that they cancelled to do this, and no one said 'no!'"

That summer, Orbison launched his first lengthy tour in decades. Then after an eight-year span without a record label, he was signed by Virgin Records. His first album consisted of re-recordings of his earlier hits. The project, *In Dreams: The Greatest Hits*, was produced by T Bone Burnett. (In the mid-1970s, Burnett was a member of Bob Dylan's legendary Rolling Thunder Revue. And it was Burnett who played a large role in Dylan's public conversion to Christianity.)

Burnett would later produce some of the tracks on Orbison's follow-up project, *Mystery Girl*, which was his first solo album of new material since the obscure *Laminar Flow* in 1979.

(Notable rock critic Dave Marsh would say of this album: "What riles me about *Laminar Flow* isn't so much that the LP is an embarrassing travesty ill-suited to one of rock's minor masters, but that such a debacle was totally unnecessary.")

One of the songs on *Mystery Girl*, "She's A Mystery," was written by U2 members Bono and the Edge. The haunting track was full of religious imagery, a hallmark of much of U2's work. Bono had been drawn to Orbison's music after hearing "In Dreams" on the *Blue Velvet* soundtrack.

The sessions for *Mystery Girl* for took longer than expected, due to producer Jeff Lynne's busy schedule. Although Orbison was enjoying some newfound success, it was Lynne's involvement with his comeback album that would lead Orbison to other musical opportunities.

▶ CHAPTER 8
GEORGE HARRISON NEEDS A B-SIDE

George Harrison's career was on fire in the late-1980s. His comeback album *Cloud Nine* was certified platinum in the U.S., and he began making a series of guest appearances on tracks for a variety of musical cohorts. He worked on sessions for longtime collaborators Gary Wright and Jim Capaldi, and even appeared on a pop hit by Belinda Carlisle, "Leave A Light On." More importantly, Harrison was finally ready to leave the safe and cloistered confines of his Friar Park estate, and had begun spending more time with friends in London and Los Angeles.

Then in a pivotal moment in rock history, Harrison needed to record a B-side track for a 12-inch single he was releasing in Europe, "This Is Love." The request for an additional track was made by his record company, Warner Brothers. The single was the followup to the hit, "When We Was Fab," and was the third release from *Cloud Nine*.

On the evening before the recording session, Harrison dined at a French restaurant in Los Angeles with Jeff Lynne, who had brought along Roy Orbison. The men spent much of their time discussing Orbison's partially-completed album. With the three legends sitting together at one table, Harrison asked Orbison and Lynne to help him to record the B-side. At first, Lynne rebuffed Harrison. But Orbison's wife, Barbara, recalled how Harrison tried another tactic: "George was very smooth. He asked Roy, 'What are you doing tomorrow?' and Roy said, 'Whatever Jeff is doing,' and George said, 'Well, I need Jeff's help.'"

For the sake of convenience, Lynne suggested they record the track at Bob Dylan's home. Harrison telephoned Dylan who agreed to the idea. Needing a guitar that he had left with Tom Petty, Harrison called and was pleasantly surprised that Petty also wanted to attend. The recording session would take place on the following day.

Dylan's home was located on a coastal bluff in an exclusive section of Malibu called Point Dume, a few hundred feet from the Pacific Ocean. The large estate featured a guard tower and various ancillary buildings. The grounds were landscaped with tropical trees and plants that were flown in from across the world when Dylan had first purchased the property.

Bill Bottrell, who engineered the session, explained: "I drove Jeff down there and we started setting up in the garage. There was all this gear Dylan had bought from Dave Stewart sitting there, not really working. Jeff and I had to quickly plug it all together and make it work as much as possible. It was hilarious. It was a real garage. You know, like Sheetrock, plasterboard walls, a metal garage door, the kind that rolls up. There may even have been lawnmowers in there. But when you've got Roy Orbison singing, the room doesn't matter. It's still going to sound like Roy." Dylan often used the garage to store a classic, cherry-red Cadillac convertible and an elaborately adorned Harley-Davidson motorcycle.

The recording session took place on April 5, 1988. Surprisingly, Dylan was late arriving for the planned session. Then, over the first two hours, Harrison and Lynne finished writing the basic music track, but none of the lyrics. Harrison had written the melody that morning.

After dining on some barbecued chicken in Dylan's backyard garden, the five assembled musicians worked out the song's lyrics. After Harrison provided the opening line, the rest of the lyrics quickly fell into place. Staring at an open box of Ampex recording tape, Harrison came up with a title for the song: "Handle With Care."

Soon after, Harrison realized the good fortune at his disposal and wanted to employ Orbison's vocals on the project. At first, Lynne thought it was a bad idea. Finally, it occurred to Harrison that all five men should sing on the track. Returning to the cluttered studio in Dylan's garage, each member of the party added their vocals to the song. Lynne would also provide the bass guitar and drum tracks. The entire writing and recording process took about five hours. Whether purposely or not, the song's opening chords were similar to the Electric Light Orchestra's 1972 track, "10538 Overture."

The following day, the 24-track tape was taken to a nearby recording studio. Heartbreakers member Mike Campbell, who was asked to play guitar on the song, recalled: "Tom called me down to the studio and they wanted to put a solo on it. So I went down there with a little Marshall amp and a Stratocaster, and Jeff (Lynne) and George (Harrison) were there. I knew them a little bit, but was pretty intimidated, coming down to play a solo with George Harrison sitting there, but I tried to put my blinders on and just do the job, so I went down there and got a sound. They played the track, and Jeff was real supportive when I played a few things, he said, 'That's the right direction,' and I played something that was a little like something Clapton might play. So I played a few things and I wasn't really thinking that it was helping the song, and George was sitting there and I said, 'Why don't you play a slide on this, because I think if you played it would be really better than what I'm doing,' and he said (nonchalantly) 'Well, OK,' he picked up the guitar with the sound that I had, and he played that amazing, beautiful solo. I was really happy that the heat was off of me."

Recording engineer Don Smith explained the song's final touches: "'Handle With Care' was finished at Westlake Audio [in Hollywood]. I had worked with Tom a lot, so he called me to come on by and just oversee what was going on. I recorded Roy's vocal [solo] 'cos he hadn't done it yet, and Tom overdubbed the harmonica because Bob didn't want to come down to the mix. And then George overdubbed his vocals. This whole thing was for a B-side. So it wasn't a big deal, and we were in there just having fun. And then all of a sudden, it's six o'clock the next morning, and they're like, 'Whoa – this is really good. You know what? This isn't just a B-side, guys.'"

When Harrison played the finished track for his record label, Warner Brothers executives Mo Ostin and Lenny Waronker were excited about what they were hearing and sensed a far bigger opportunity. The label was also concerned that the 12-inch single might be imported into the U.S. and would take away from the album's sales – especially since the track wasn't included on *Cloud Nine*.

With the label bosses encouraging Harrison and the other four rock legends to regroup and record an entire album, it seemed as if everything was falling into place. But Harrison was already enjoying a significant comeback with the release of his solo album, *Cloud Nine*, and was apprehensive about taking on a major side project. Finally, Harrison was persuaded after Ostin argued that an all-star album would provide the former Beatle with another creative outlet and could potentially become a sizable career boost. Harrison recalled, "The record company said, 'Oh, we can't put that out, it's too good!' So I thought, 'Well, we'll just have to do another nine songs and make an album.'"

Music critic Terry Staunton would say of the track: "What starts as a typically well-crafted Harrisonesque lament is elevated to pop glory by Orbison's voice on the bridge. But [it] doesn't stop there. Dylan weighs in on a second bridge, and it's plain to see that we're listening to something very special. And let's not undervalue Lynne or Petty's contributions." Ironically, what was intended as a disposable B-side would soon become the memorable opening track of a hit album.

A week after "Handle With Care" was recorded, Harrison asked the other four musicians who played on the track if they would be interested in forming a band. Jeff Lynne, who had been encouraging Harrison to start a new group, was the first to join. Next up, Petty and then Dylan both agreed to participate.

(Lynne did not think Dylan would agree to be part of the project.)

Petty recalled how the group's lineup was finalized: "We all jumped in a car to go see Roy play [at the Celebrity Theatre] in Anaheim. We ran into Roy's dressing room, threw everybody out and said, 'We want you to be in our band, Roy.' He said, 'That'd be great,' then gave this unbelievable show." Harrison had made the proposal official by dropping to his knees and formally asking Orbison to join the band.

The five men soon celebrated the birth of their new venture with a band meeting – not at a fancy nightclub or high-priced bistro – but at a Denny's restaurant on Sunset Boulevard in Hollywood.

Despite the fact that Orbison was in the middle of a tour, he made time for the project. Petty was also forced to put aside his solo album for the moment. Dylan, meanwhile, needed to prepare for an upcoming tour and practice with his new backing band, and could devote only a limited number of days to recording the album.

George Harrison's wife, Olivia, recounted the origin of the band's quirky name: "[George] and Jeff used to call gadgets in the studio 'wilburys,' like, 'Let's give that sound a trembling wilbury.'" But while Harrison had originally wanted to call the group the Trembling Wilburys, Lynne intervened and the two men settled on the Traveling Wilburys.

Although all five members of the group were individually signed to various labels, the project went forward as planned without any contractual glitches. As Orbison explained at the time, "We didn't ask any of the record companies or [any] manager or attorneys or anybody. We just went ahead and did it and no one knew about it. It was right in the middle of my album with five songs recorded and five to go. We just kept it a secret until the writing and singing was done and then we mentioned it to all the record companies, to CBS, Warner, Virgin and MCA, who all said no problem, which was great. I think if we had tried to get together and told everyone that we were forming a little group they would have told us that there were too many problems. I remember one executive said, 'Well, I'm not going to stand in the way of history,' and just hung up the phone."

The new group crafted the bulk of the album at Dave Stewart's estate, atop Coldwater Canyon in the Encino Hills section of Los Angeles. The recording sessions took place during a sunny stretch of great Southern California weather. George Harrison was actually living at Stewart's home for a period of time before the album was even planned.

Stewart was very good friends with most of the Traveling Wilburys, particularly Tom Petty. Stewart and Petty had met for the first time at the Sunset Sound recording studio in Hollywood. After a Eurythmics concert in May 1984, Stewart wanted to discuss some unfinished songs with producer Jimmy Iovine, who at the time was working on Stevie Nicks' third solo album. Out of the blue, Iovine decided he needed Petty's input. Taking a much needed break from the arduous recording sessions in his basement studio, Petty was happy to meet with

Iovine. Arriving at Sunset Sound, Petty instantly clicked with Stewart. The feeling was mutual, with Stewart recalling, "Tom Petty came down and he was truly the coolest cat I'd ever met. We hit it off immediately."

While sharing a bottle of aged whiskey, the two men quickly completed Stewart's unfinished composition, "Don't Come Around Here No More." Stewart had intended to give the track to Stevie Nicks. But after Petty contributed some of the lyrics, he came to realize that he wanted the song for himself. Stewart recalled the tense situation: "He said to Jimmy, 'I think I should sing this song,' and then they started having a kind of [argument] amongst themselves – well not a real [argument], but a strange conversation. Tom and Stevie had done a duet of Tom's song called 'Stop Draggin' My Heart Around,' and Jimmy had put it on Stevie's album. It was a huge success for her, but not for him as it kinda stopped his album in its tracks. I think Tom saw history repeating itself and decided he wanted to put this one on his album."

Stewart later admitted, "The reason why I built a house and a studio in America, in Los Angeles, was because I became very good friends with Tom. I didn't really know anybody else. But he seemed so real. About four streets away I bought some property. George Harrison and his wife would stay there. I was also spending some time with Dylan. I seemed to have a link with Dylan and then Tom Petty. And then George Harrison. You could kind of see the Wilburys coming together."

Over the next few years, Petty and Stewart became very close. In fact, the two men hosted many parties at Petty's home during the mid-1980s.

Stewart had first met Dylan in the mid-1980s: "I'd agreed to produce Feargal Sharkey's solo album, his first departure from the pop-punk band the Undertones.... On the second day of recording, I was at the mixing desk when the studio receptionist rang through and said, 'I have Bob Dylan on the phone for you.' My first reaction was that this was Feargal messing around. I answered saying, 'Ha, Feargal. Great joke!' But when I heard the voice on the other end of the line, it was unmistakable. After years of hearing this voice come out of my dad's gramophone and every stereo I ever owned, learning his songs over and over and spending nights just discussing every nuance of a Dylan song, I was now connected to him by this twisted wire. Every word was like an electric shock to my brain. In fact, all I can remember is Dylan saying something like, 'Do you wanna meet up and talk about films and stuff?'"

During a subsequent conversation, Dylan made an admission. As Stewart later recalled, "Bob Dylan had told me back in 1984, way before the Wilburys. That he'd love to have a band again that felt like a real band. I said, 'the only band like that is the Heartbreakers.'"

Stewart's lush, hillside estate was full of breezy trees and exotic vegetation, and was an ideal spot for the creative process. Inside the main house, there was a grand piano in the living room and most of the furnishings were decorated in relaxing, off-white, pastel hues. The estate also had a tennis court, and Harrison and Petty often played matches against each other. There was also an inviting swimming pool on the property.

Stewart would describe his home as a miraculous place: "I

built that house from scratch, and it seemed to be built on some kind of fault line or maybe some magic energy, which Encino has from the Native American settlements. I don't know what it was, but it just became this place where everybody was in my back garden. I suppose it was because I was hooked into it all and I met each one of these people individually, and so it was the obvious meeting place. 'Hey, let's go around Dave's!' It's a funny thing, when you're in that situation."

The recording studio was set up in Stewart's guest house – an unassuming Spanish-style, wood-framed cottage – which was situated in a relaxed, wooded yard. The building had a comfortable porch which featured a swinging bench and a large punching bag dangling from the ceiling.

Stewart later recalled, "It was kind of weird to look out my back window and see Bob Dylan, Roy Orbison, Tom Petty, George Harrison and Jeff Lynne strumming their guitars sitting on the grass under a tree." Stewart, who had prior commitments in England with the Eurythmics, left shortly after the start of the recording sessions.

The album was recorded over a short period in early May, with the daily recording sessions following a regular routine. The five members of the group would usually arrive at noon or 1PM, and then begin socializing around a large pot of coffee in the home's relatively small kitchen. There were just five chairs set up in the room. Lynne and Orbison were usually the first to arrive, with Orbison often bringing cakes for lunch. On one day, Lynne showed up wearing a Tom Petty concert t-shirt.

With the sessions usually ending around midnight, the five men would unwind by having a few beers, informally playing music or exchanging stories before going home. In the Martin Scorsese film, *George Harrison: Living In The Material World*, the Wilburys are seen playing the 1950s standard, "(Ghost) Riders In The Sky." On some nights, Harrison would pass around ukeleles to his bandmates.

As for non-musical entertainment, two members of the group – Orbison and Harrison – could both recite and perform complete skits from *Monty Python's Flying Circus*.

Needing a drummer, the group brought in Jim Keltner, who was later given the nickname, Buster Sidebury. Keltner had previously worked with Tom Petty, toured and recorded with Dylan, had toured or recorded with three of the four Beatles, and performed at George Harrison's charity event, the Concert for Bangladesh. In addition to Keltner – who would also appear in the band's music videos – other guest musicians at the sessions included sax player Jim Horn and percussionists Ray Cooper and Ian Wallace (who played the tom-toms on "Handle With Care").

The only non-musicians who regularly visited the sessions were Alan "Bugs" Weidel, Petty's longtime roadie and guitar tech, and Victor Maymudes, a member of Dylan's road crew. (The wives of Harrison and Orbison also made a few appearances.)

Surprisingly, it was not a challenge for the five individual rock stars to put aside their personal egos for the sake of the album. Harrison emerged as the chief Wilbury, pushing and prodding his bandmates during the entire creative process. Although Harrison was in charge, Lynne recalled: "I think everybody was kind of looking up to Bob. He didn't take any leadership role, he just wanted to be one of the lads. He actually wanted to call the band Roy And The Boys."

Harrison's wife, Olivia, explained the lighthearted nature of the sessions: "George was kind of the kingpin, the driving force. 'Come on, let's have some fun.' I didn't see any ego. I think all of them transcended that. If you can't be satisfied at that point in your life then you've got a problem. Nobody was there to try and prove anything."

Of the five Wilburys, Petty at age 38 was by far the youngest member of the group, while Orbison, at 52, was the oldest. Petty later recalled, "Well, they treated me equally, which was nice. But I always felt like I was the kid in the band. I was the one who was really lucky to be there. But they never treated me that way."

With Dylan scheduled to begin a solo tour, it was imperative that the sessions were completed on time. "We got everyone to agree and did the other nine [songs] the same way, writing them like we had to be done tomorrow," Harrison recalled.

Most of the tracks written in an informal environment in Stewart's kitchen or living room. Petty explained the process: "We'd start out every day in the living room of the main house, tossing lines out." Some of the members – like Harrison and Petty – had lots of experience co-writing songs, while others – like Dylan and Orbison – considered the process of songwriting to be a solitary task. Dylan explained: "Outside of writing with the Traveling Wilburys, my shared experience writing a song with other songwriters is not that great. Of course, unless you find the right person to write with as a partner.... you're awfully lucky if you do, but if you don't, it's really more trouble than it's worth, trying to write something with somebody."

When the writing was done, the five men would head to the guest house and record multiple takes of the track to determine whose voice best suited the particular song. One music critic noted: "In almost every song, however, someone other than the lead makes a significant solo contribution, and a couple are true ensemble numbers, with solos handed around and more inventive harmony singing than the latter-day incarnation of Crosby, Stills, Nash & Young can muster."

As for settling disagreements, Petty recalled, "We usually went by a group decision. We were pretty honest with each other. In recording or writing, when somebody gets the right part, everybody knows." Although the entire group was credited with writing the songs, some of the individual members brought in their own partially-completed compositions.

The group used a basic 24-track mixing board, with Lynne usually at the controls. With a slew of wires leading to the control room, the five men sat in a circle as they played their acoustic guitars. Petty and Orbison – both heavy smokers – would usually sit next to each other and share an ashtray on the floor. With the two men becoming close friends, Orbison would soon begin calling Petty by his nickname, "Tommy." At one point in the sessions, Jim Keltner tapped his drumsticks on a refrigerator to get the right sound.

After the musical tracks were completed, the members of the band usually went out to dinner at a local restaurant, where they would work out some of the lyrics.

Remarkably, the tracks were written and recorded in just ten days. Meanwhile, when Dave Stewart returned from England, he was hoping to observe some of the sessions but was surprised to discover that the album had already been finished.

After taking a one-week break, Harrison and Lynne headed to London – with master tapes in hand – to clean up and tweak the songs at Harrison's personal home studio – named FPSHOT (Friar Park Studio, Henley-on-Thames).

Friar Park was an exquisite 62-acre estate located 30-miles west of London. It was built in the 19th century by an eccentric lawyer named Sir Frank Crisp and had been purchased by Harrison in 1970. At the time, it was in a state of disrepair and was scheduled to be demolished.

Over the next decade, Harrison would spend a great deal of time and resources repairing the structures and restoring the numerous gardens. The 120-room Victorian-era, neo-Gothic home resembled a royal castle, a fitting abode for a former Beatle. The cover of Harrison's album, *All Things Must* Pass, was photographed on the lawn of the estate and his 1976 hit "Crackerbox Palace" was a homage to his home. And track, "Ballad Of Sir Frankie Crisp (Let It Roll)" chronicled the history of the estate. Harrison would once describe Crisp as a cross between Walt Disney and Lewis Carroll.

Harrison and Lynne were later joined in the control room by Petty and Orbison. When crafting music, Harrison was known as a perfectionist. His longtime collaborator Gary Wright explained, "There was no room in his personality for 'that's good enough;' he carried his ideas to their unique fulfillment."

Harrison had constructed his recording studio in 1971, with a then state-of-the-art, 16-track mixing board and Altec speakers. The custom-built studio had been designed by Eddie Veale, who had previously constructed a studio for John Lennon. Harrison later installed a 24-track board.

Beginning in 1974, FPSHOT was the recording base for Harrison's new label, Dark Horse Records. He would record most of his solo albums at the studio, beginning with *Living In The Material World*.

A mere six-weeks from the start of the sessions, the album was completed. Through it all, the members of the Traveling Wilburys had somehow managed to keep news of the project from their friends, colleagues and even the rock press. (*Rolling Stone* magazine had not written anything about the group until a few weeks *after* the release of the album.)

It was Harrison who first leaked the news about his all-star band. On the February 10 episode of the syndicated radio show *Rockline*, he told host Bob Coburn about the new project: "It's this new group I got – it's called the Traveling Wilburys. I'd like to do an album with them and later we can all do our own albums again."

Meanwhile, a few weeks after the Wilburys album was completed, Dylan released his 25th studio album, *Down In The Groove*. One of the poorest sellers of his career, he was hoping for a sales boost following his extended tour with the Heartbreakers. Then a week later, Dylan launched "The

Interstate 88 Tour," which would soon be renamed "The Never Ending Tour," as the folk-rock legend would remain on the road for the next three decades.

Meanwhile, Orbison began rehearsals for an upcoming European concert in the spring, followed by a planned U.S. tour in the summer.

▶ CHAPTER 9
VOLUME ONE

After the completed Traveling Wilburys album was delivered to Warner Brothers, the label did not have high hopes for a project that was recorded by five older musicians, quickly and cheaply. With some members of the group refusing to consider a tour to publicize and promote the album, Warner Brothers initially neglected to spend any real money on trade ads, radio spots or record store promotions.

Michael Palin – a well-respected British comedian and member of the Monty Python comedy troupe – was hired by Harrison to write the band's fictional biography. Using the pseudonym Hugh Jampton, Palin chronicled the short story of five half-brothers who had one father, but five different mothers. He wrote: "Each of the five mythical Wilburys was born to a different wife of the same father, Charles Truscott Wilbury, Sr., a notorious drinker and womanizer."

Consequently, all five members of the group decided to use aliases. Their real names did not appear anywhere on the album or cover. While Petty took the name Charlie T. Wilbury, Jr., the other members emerged as Otis (Jeff Lynne), Lucky (Bob Dylan), Nelson (George Harrison) and Lefty (Roy Orbison). Meanwhile, *New York Times* reviewer John Rockwell wrote: "Their 'anonymity' is just pretense, since they allow their photo to appear on the jacket and their voices are recognizable. Some have suggested that record-company conflicts were a reason for the ruse. But the various companies are still credited, and the most likely explanation is sheer self-amusement."

Released on October 18, 1988, *The Traveling Wilburys, Vol. 1* was met by mostly positive reviews in the rock press. *Rolling Stone* gave the project four stars and declared, "This is the best record of its kind ever made. Then again, this is the only record of its kind ever made. A low-key masterpiece, *Volume One* marks the auspicious debut of the Traveling Wilburys.... One of the few rock supergroups actually deserving to be called either super or a group." Some reviewers were critical of the upbeat nature of the tracks and were hoping for a more serious and cerebral project. One critic, Steve Morse, of *The Boston Globe*, was far more dismissive of the project: "It may not prove to be more than a footnote item in each artist's career.... It's a corny concept – and not all of the music survives the silliness."

The front cover of the album was highlighted by the group's distinctive retro-style logo and a simple but artsy black-and-white collage of the five musicians, while the back cover featured an image of five well-worn and traveled guitar cases. Surprisingly, Harrison was not the focus of the artwork, since he was the defacto leader of the group.

Almost immediately, the album exploded on the charts.

What Warner Brothers failed to grasp was that each of the group's five members had their own loyal followings. And it also helped that the album contained a number of well-written, hook-filled songs. The album's first release, "Handle With Care," enjoyed heavy airplay on AOR stations and was a turntable hit on top-40 radio, with the single stalling out at #45 on the charts. Selling more than two-million copies in the U.S. during its first year of release, the album was also a strong seller around the world, particularly in Australia and Canada.

The song's music video was filmed in Los Angeles, inside a large, airy, empty warehouse with a high ceiling. It was directed by David Leland, who had also worked with Tom Petty. In the video, the five members of the group stood in a circle, singing and strumming their guitars, while facing a solitary, overhead, vintage microphone. While Harrison appeared particularly happy, Orbison looked a bit tense.

Also, Harrison was playing a Gretsch electric guitar embossed with a Traveling Wilburys logo, which he had commissioned. (Soon after, Gretsch introduced several models of Traveling Wilburys guitars, which featured the stamped autographs of the band members on the back.)

Lynne recalled the lighthearted atmosphere among his bandmates after the filming was completed: "I'll never forget being in the van leaving the location of the video shoot... Roy was doing a Monty Python sketch, playing all the parts himself, which was really funny, then he started giggling. This giggle was totally infectious and the more he did it the more we couldn't resist. I still have the picture in my mind of George Harrison, Bob Dylan, Tom Petty and me all giggling like a bunch of schoolgirls along with Roy Orbison."

The album's second single, "End Of The Line" – which was primarily written by George Harrison – combined elements of the British skiffle movement of Harrison's teen years with the folk-rock stylings of 1960s-era Dylan. Harrison came up with the basic chords, Petty and Dylan added to the melody and the rest of the band wrote the lyrics. Every member, except for Dylan, performed a vocal solo on the song.

The music video for the track was filmed just four days after the sudden death of Roy Orbison and just three weeks after the album's release. The five members of the band were scheduled to film two music videos at a production studio near London.

The video for "End Of The Line" was shot inside a vintage passenger car on a moving train. During Orbison's vocal solos, the camera focused on a framed portrait of the singer, which was perched near a weathered rocking chair that held a resting, upright guitar. Dylan reluctantly appeared at the video and reportedly angered the rest of the group by leaving early. (The song was later featured in the 1989, George Harrison-produced comedy film, *Checking Out.*)

Around this time, three members of the Wilburys – Petty, Harrison and Lynne – promoted the album with an appearance on MTV. But Harrison dominated the interview with the announcement that he was retiring. During the 19-minute segment, an overly-relaxed Petty was happy to sit quietly off to the side, where he eventually began snacking on an apple. Meanwhile, Dylan was being the classic Dylan and chose not to give interviews to promote the project. In fact, he rarely granted any interviews to the press in the latter part of his career.

Over the next year, the album would continue to garner heavy airplay on AOR radio with tracks such as "Last Night," "Heading For The Light" and "Tweeter And The Monkey Man." Harrison recalled what went into making the latter track: "'Tweeter And The Monkey Man' began with Tom and Bob sitting around in the kitchen, talking about all this stuff which didn't make much sense to me. I think it's Americana stuff. We got a cassette tape, put it on, then transcribed everything they were saying and then Bob changed it. That, for me, was just amazing to watch." The song was recorded in only two takes and was the only track on the album that did not feature Orbison on vocals.

"Tweeter And The Monkey Man" was also notable for its many references to Bruce Springsteen songs. Ironically, early in his career, Springsteen was branded in the press as the "New Dylan." (Conversely, Roy Orbison was mentioned in the lyrics of the Springsteen song, "Thunder Road.")

Another strong track, "Not Alone Anymore," featured only Orbison on vocals and harked back to his 1960s period of tear-jerker ballads about heartache and loneliness. As Lynne recalled: "When Roy came to sing 'Not Alone Anymore,' everybody just sat there going, 'Wow! It's Roy Orbison.' Even though he's become your pal and hanging out and having a laugh and going to dinner, as soon as he gets behind that mike, and doing his business, suddenly it's shudder time." But Lynne was not satisfied with the song's musical accompaniment, so he took it upon himself to re-record the musical portion of the song during a solitary, late-night session.

The Traveling Wilburys managed two unexpected honors in *Rolling Stone* magazine's 1988 annual readers poll. The group scored the #10 Best Album of the Year and was ranked #2 in the category of Best New American Band, right behind Guns N' Roses. Also, the group won the Album of the Year prize in the inaugural International Rock Awards.

With the group's unforeseen success, Harrison began contemplating the possibility of a Wilburys "adventure film," reminiscent of the early Beatles movie, *A Hard Day's Night*. The project would have been handled by Harrison's production company, Handmade Films, which he established in 1978 with his business manager, Denis O'Brien, to produce the comedy spoof *Monty Python's Life Of Brian*. In order to finance the Monty Python film, Harrison had mortgaged his 120-room estate. Over the next ten years, the company produced nearly two-dozen films, including the 1986 Madonna box-office bomb, *Shanghai Surprise*. (In 1994, Harrison would sell his stake in the business for a mere $8.5 million.)

Although the Wilburys had surprised both themselves and their record company with a commercially successful project, the members were uncertain at this point whether or not to regroup for a second album. As Petty explained at the time, "Though we've all said we'd do it again, I would hate to see it become too official. Then it would be like work."

▶ CHAPTER 10
PETTY: SONGS FROM THE GARAGE

Prior to forming the Traveling Wilburys, Tom Petty had been working on his first solo album, which was tentatively titled *Songs From The Garage*. Not surprisingly, Petty's two side projects were causing some tensions inside the Heartbreakers camp: "I think there was some confusion about it. They didn't know what I was doing, especially after I joined the Wilburys. They were probably ticked off for a while. I don't know because they're not really the kind of people who will call you up and tell you how they're feeling. They just kind of disappeared." But Petty was also disheartened by the lack of positive feedback or support for his solo album from his bandmates. As Petty recalled, "[Benmont Tench] used to say, 'Oh, I liked that song, 'Free Fallin'.' I think that's really good.' [But] none of them ever came up and said, 'Hey, great album!'"

But Petty's bandmates were not alone in failing to grasp the album's potential. After playing the completed tracks for the label bosses at MCA, Petty was shocked when the project was panned and passed over for release. Petty later recalled: "It's the only time in my life that a record's been rejected. And I was stunned. And I was so high on the record, and I tried to think, 'What did I do wrong?' They said they didn't hear any hits, and there turned out to be, like, four or five hits on the record, some of the biggest ones I ever had." Remaining optimistic, Petty recounted, "I carried a tape around and played it for everyone. And everybody liked it except the record company. They were quizzical. They were the last ones I was able to convert." Convinced that the record executives at MCA were dead wrong, Petty simply waited them out. In the interim, he decided to add a few more tracks to the album.

On January 6, 1989, at the Ventura Theatre near Los Angeles, Petty was a surprise guest at a concert by a new lineup of the Byrds, which featured Roger McGuinn, David Crosby, and Chris Hillman. Petty joined the three rock legends for a performance of "So You Wanna Be A Rock 'n' Roll Star." Hillman recalled: "We had Tom Petty on rhythm guitar that night! He based his whole musical career on the Byrds, and took it to another level." Just days after the concert, Petty was inspired to record a rendition of the Byrds' classic "Feel A Whole Lot Better" for inclusion on his solo album. Petty recalled, "My daughter thought I wrote it. And I played it for [Roger] McGuinn and he said, 'Is that us?'"

Finally, when the old regime at MCA had been replaced, Petty returned with his solo album. This time, the new management team loved the songs and Petty was vindicated.

Released in April 1989, *Full Moon Fever* was a huge smash. Remarkably, eight of the album's twelve tracks received airplay

72

on rock radio. But the initial reviews were not entirely positive. A *Rolling Stone* critic said of the album, "*Full Moon Fever* isn't Petty's best record."

Explaining the upbeat nature of his solo album, Petty admitted that losing his home in a devastating fire and nearly perishing were transforming experiences: "My life changed, the whole tone of my music changed. That anger went away. You hear *Full Moon Fever* – it's a very happy, pleasant and positive album and was meant to be so. And that was a result of just being so glad to be alive." Additionally, *Full Moon Fever* veered from the traditional Heartbreakers sound with its subdued drums, scarcity of keyboards, and prominent use of acoustic guitars. Although *Full Moon Fever* was considered a solo work, all of the Heartbreakers except for drummer Stan Lynch performed on the album. Additionally, every member of the Traveling Wilburys had appeared on the album, except for Bob Dylan.

The first single, "I Won't Back Down," was a multi-format hit. The track featured what Petty described as an "acoustic wall of sound.... There were four of us – myself, Mike, Jeff and George – playing acoustic [guitars] live in the studio. One guitar was a 12-string, two were probably six strings and one was Nashville strung. Then we doubled the parts so we had eight acoustics playing the rhythm parts, which created this huge sound." But there was an unexpected issue with Campbell's performance. He played "a deeply inspired, very Harrison-esque slide solo on this tune. In fact, the solo was almost left on the mixing room floor for sounding too much like Harrison."

Meanwhile, Petty scored a major coup when he wrangled half of the Beatles to appear in the song's music video. Flying to England to film the clip, Petty was joined by George Harrison, Ringo Starr, Jeff Lynne, and Mike Campbell. When Harrison arrived at the video shoot, he came bearing gifts and handed everyone in the band a vintage Beatles watch from the 1960s. Petty recalled, "It was George's idea to get Ringo. What am I going to say – No? I knew Ringo. He would hang around with us. But I still can't believe that happened. We had amps on the set, and we'd be jamming between takes. I remember playing and looking at Mike, like, 'How about this?'"

On the second day of the video shoot, director David Leland realized he needed one more shot of Ringo. But after the former Beatle had been told he wouldn't be needed on that day, the panicked director was forced to use a "replacement" Ringo from the Beatlemania stage show. (In the video, Campbell played the vintage Fender Stratocaster guitar that Harrison had used in the 1967 Beatles film, *Magical Mystery Tour*.)

Over the next 18 months, *Full Moon Fever* would continue to generate additional radio hits including "Love Is A Long Road," "A Face In The Crowd," and a song inspired by a group of young punks that Petty had encountered in a Los Angeles diner, "Zombie Zoo." The latter track featured backing vocals by Roy Orbison.

While Petty was recording the last few songs of his solo album, he found himself in the same studio as Orbison. During this period, Heartbreakers guitarist Mike Campbell was producing some of Orbison's tracks for his comeback album.

Having been apart from some of the Heartbreakers for a full

two years, Petty had to reacquaint himself with some of his longtime bandmates. Missing from the once close-knit outfit was the daily social interaction among the members, who were now fully immersed in their own separate ventures.

Because *Full Moon Fever* was considered a solo Petty project, the members of the Heartbreakers had to learn how to play the songs after the album was released. The group's drummer Stan Lynch complained at the time: "That was the first time a tour ever felt like work to me – I never want to feel like I'm in a cover band."

At this point in his career, Petty was at the top of his game. In addition to nearly 15 years worth of Heartbreakers standards, he possessed a potent musical catalog that included hit songs from both the Traveling Wilburys and his very successful solo album. But at a time when Petty should have been basking in glory, he was forced to battle an unexpected problem. Petty explained: "For the first time in my career, I developed stage fright. After a whole career in which I was very happy to take the stage, all of a sudden I went through a period of being terrified, puking, the whole thing."

Meanwhile, in April 1989, Dylan would release his 26th studio album, *Oh Mercy*. Taking advice from U2's Bono to work with producer Daniel Lanois, Dylan returned to form and released his most critically-acclaimed solo album since the late-1970s.

✦ ✧ ✦ ✧ ✦

With the Strange Behavior tour scheduled to end in mid-September, the members of the Heartbreakers pressured Tom Petty to add more dates. But Petty had other plans. As music writer Bill Flanagan reported at the time: "The Heartbreakers want to stay on the road, strike while the iron is hot, but Petty has decided not to extend the tour. Tom wants to take a break to write. The original plan was for the band to record a new album from late '89 to early '90.... But no one expected *Full Moon Fever* to be such a smash. Now the Heartbreakers want to keep working, but Tom sees no reason to push it.... The underlying fear among the Heartbreakers is that if they quit touring now, Tom will get caught up with the Wilburys again, which will lead God-knows where for God-knows how long, and another year will be lost."

Meanwhile, Petty continued to remain evasive about a possible, second Traveling Wilburys album: "We don't have any plans at the moment to do anything. We're not ruling out that we might do another one. At the moment, we're all catching up with everything else that we put on hold to do the Wilburys. So if we get time one day, I wouldn't rule it out, but at the moment, there's no telling if it'll ever happen again. And, of course, Roy's death was a wrench in the works. There was something in that particular chemistry of people, those five guys, that was real magical. So for the time being, we'll just remain friends and stay in touch and we'll see one day where it goes."

In press interviews, the members of the Wilburys also

remained noncommittal about whether or not the group would tour. Harrison told one interviewer: "I've always played around in my own mind with what a Wilburys tour could be. Would each person do a solo set and then do Wilburys at the end, or would we all go on right from beginning to end and make everything Wilburys? It's an intriguing thought.... We could all sing 'Blowin' In The Wind,' and Bob could sing 'Something.'"

Eventually, the four members of the Wilburys met with a major promoter who offered a very large guarantee for a short tour. Although Petty and Lynne were definitely up for the project, Dylan and Harrison remained on the fence. Petty recalled, "A lot of money was offered to us, but at the end of the meeting, we'd decided not to do it. And I kept getting down on my knees in front of George, saying, 'Please! It's so much money.' And everybody would just start laughing. It was that kind of meeting; we'd look at each other and start giggling nervously, going, 'Nah, we can't.' Like George says, I can't see waking up in a hotel in Philadelphia and having to do a Wilburys sound check."

In the end, it was Harrison who ultimately nixed the tour. At that point in his life, the former Beatle enjoyed remaining in the shadows and saw no reason to launch a tour, which would have turned into an overblown media spectacle.

Alternatively, Petty offered the musical services of the Heartbreakers for a solo Harrison tour. But nothing came of that, either.

At the beginning of 1990, Petty wanted to start working on a new Heartbreakers album, but was forced to delay his plans after learning that Jeff Lynne was in the middle of his own solo project. Instead, Petty asked the Heartbreakers to go back on the road. With *Full Moon Fever* continuing to rack up massive sales, Petty recalled that "promoters kept calling and calling."

▶ CHAPTER 11
ROY ORBISON: IN DREAMS

Roy Orbison was experiencing a major career revival during the late 1980s. After a Chicago concert in March 1988, a reviewer wrote, "At first glance, it seems rather difficult to explain the rapturous response rock pioneer Roy Orbison received Tuesday night when he performed at the Riviera Club. The audience was up and cheering before he was barely on stage.... Throughout the hourlong greatest-hits set Tuesday night, the ovations would come again and again."

Orbison stated at the time, "I've been rediscovered by young kids who had never heard of me before the Wilburys. They are getting into my original songs, and apparently the old stuff is selling at the rate of 20,000 copies a day. It's very nice to be wanted again, but I still can't quite believe it." During this period, Orbison was also planning to start work on his long planned autobiography, which he had hoped to turn into a feature film.

In November, Orbison traveled to Europe to accept an

award. While there, he also shot footage for his "You Got It" video at the Diamond Awards Festival in Antwerp, Belgium. It would mark his first and only public performance of the song. Looking more like rock star than at any time in his career, he dominated the large stage as the spellbound audience knew they were witnessing something special. Although he appeared confident and at ease, Orbison clearly looked pale. After returning to the U.S. for a concert in Boston, he began preparing for a video shoot with the Traveling Wilburys.

Then on December 4, Orbison performed for a packed house at the Front Row Theater in suburban Cleveland. At the concert, he fired on all cylinders. Looking thin, dressed in black and sporting a tied-back pony tail, Orbison was still doing his regular 50 to 60 minute set of his classic, older material, and did not perform any tracks from the Traveling Wilburys or his new solo album. He closed the concert with the ballad, "Running Scared."

Orbison's son, Alex, recalled that his father "talked about intensive rehearsals in January '89 that he was going to do with his band to combine the old material with the new material." He had also planned to dramatically extend the length of his concerts. Orbison also spoke to his band and family about inviting the various members of the Wilburys to join him on stage during his upcoming tour. He was hoping to somehow wrangle all four of his bandmates to one show.

Flying to Hendersonville, Tennessee – which is just outside of Nashville – Orbison needed to unwind before beginning a grueling series of press interviews, band rehearsals and overseas video shoots that were scheduled over the next few months. There, he met with his mother and sons.

On the second day of his short break, Orbison spent much of the afternoon at the home of Grand Ole Opry singer Jean Shepard. Her husband, Benny Birchfield, was Orbison's longtime tour bus driver. After going into town to buy parts for his model airplanes, Orbison spent a few hours flying the small crafts in Shepard's back yard.

After going home, Orbison collapsed in his mother's bathroom at around 10PM. He had suffered a fatal heart attack. Although he had complained of chest pains over the previous month – mentioning the discomfort to his close friend Johnny Cash – Orbison had not taken the symptoms seriously. According to Sun Records founder Sam Phillips, Orbison's son "Wesley had spoken to his dad just a few hours before he died and said he hadn't sounded that happy in a long time."

The New York Times incorrectly reported in an obituary: "Mr. Orbison gave [his final] concert Sunday in Akron, Ohio, before 2,000 people." And the tabloid, *The National Enquirer*, ran a front-page headline suggesting that Orbison had worked himself to death – which wasn't that much of a stretch. Although he appeared healthy, Orbison's quick 30-pound weight loss over the previous several months had weakened his heart.

The sudden death of Orbison would hit his Wilburys bandmates hard. Petty stated at the time: "The way Roy saw life and just enjoyed it so much, it just brought home to me that you're only given so many heartbeats and you'd better use every one." But Petty would later reveal, "I always felt like he was very prepared to go, spiritually and mentally. He was in a very good place, spiritually, and I don't think death would've freaked him at all. So I always felt comforted by that, and by the fact that he got a lot of attention, at least in the Wilburys – everyone was always hugging him and telling him how much they loved him. And I'm glad we did."

Lynne later recalled his reaction to Orbison's death: "That was devastating because it was so sudden. He had a heart attack and was gone. He just checked out. We'd just worked together on 'You Got It'... and it had been his first top five hit in 30 years. It was still in the charts when he died. He'd been so happy." Amazingly, the track was also a big hit on AOR radio, which was a confirmation of his renewed popularity.

However, Orbison's personal life had been marred by tragedy over the years. His first wife Claudette – who was the inspiration for his 1964 hit "Oh, Pretty Woman" – died in his arms after a motorcycle accident. Two years later, his house was destroyed in a fire that also took the lives of two of his three young sons. From that point forward, Orbison promised himself he would never attend another funeral.

In 1987, Orbison countered: "People seem to dwell on those tragedies. People always say 'Poor thing, he lost his wife and kids.' Well, that was twenty years ago. I've been married to my second wife Barbara for eighteen years now. Sure, that was a rough time, but I think that everyone has them. OK, mine were especially large tragedies, especially within a two-year period. But there's nothing I've gone through that nobody else won't go through."

A chain smoker who underwent triple-bypass surgery, Orbison was not blessed with good health. While taping a performance at the Liberty Bowl in 1978, he experienced dizziness while running up the bleachers. Orbison recalled: "I was lucky. Without immediate attention I could have had a massive coronary. I didn't ask the doctors about my chances. I said, 'Let's just get it on'." According to *People* magazine, Roy said to his doctor: "'Make sure it's a clean, pretty incision. I perform with my shirts open pretty far down.' She thought I was completely bonkers."

But in a profession where drug and alcohol use were practically mandatory, tobacco was Orbison's only vice. According to Orbison's biographer John Kruth, when Orbison was still a boy, "Roy's father, Orbie Lee had steered him clear for any taste for alcohol. Seeing his dad with a glass of bourbon in his hand one day, Roy asked what he was drinking. 'And he told me, and I said, 'Can I have some?' And he said sure. So I slugged back a big shot of whiskey and I think I was sick for about six days. So that turned me off of drink forever. I still don't drink.'"

Although he tried giving up cigarettes for a brief period after his heart surgery, Orbison was not successful. Ironically, at the time of is death, he had been on a serious diet and looked thinner and healthier than he had in decades. He appeared significantly heavier on stage at his *A Black & White Night* concert, which was shot just 14 months earlier. Photographs from Orbison's final concert showed him smiling, relaxed and looking very fit.

Just weeks before his death, he was asked by a *Rolling Stone* interviewer if he "felt healthy." He responded, "Yeah, yeah. Having lost a little weight, and my blood pressure's right with the diet... And working out with the trainer from time to time. Everything's terrific. Couldn't be better."

Two tributes were held for Orbison, the first in Nashville. Then on February 24, 1990, a second tribute was staged at the Universal Amphitheatre in Los Angeles. Bob Dylan was the biggest name at the event, and was joined by three members of the Byrds – Chris Hillman, David Crosby and Roger McGuinn – on an extended rendition of "Mr. Tambourine Man." The four men followed up with a performance of "He Was A Friend Of Mine," a folk standard that deals with the death of a close friend.

Also appearing on the bill were Iggy Pop, John Lee Hooker, John Fogerty, the Stray Cats, B.B. King, Bonnie Raitt, and Orbison's former collaborator k.d. lang. The concert was broadcast on Showtime with the proceeds going to a homeless charity. Surprisingly, Dylan was the only surviving Wilburys member at the tribute. (Petty was also scheduled to appear but was a no-show.)

Also on the bill was Orbison's musical progeny, a relatively unknown singer named Chris Isaak, who would score his first hit the following year with the haunting ballad, "Wicked Game." The oddest performance of the night was actor Dean Stockwell's lip-syncing rendition of "In Dreams," which he had famously mimed in the film, *Blue Velvet*. For an encore, Dylan was joined by a number of musical guests on the Orbison standard, "Only The Lonely."

After his death, Orbison became the first musical act since Elvis Presley in 1977 to land two posthumous albums in the Top-5, with *The Traveling Wilburys, Vol. 1* and his solo venture, *Mystery Girl*. In the U.K., Orbison would manage to place two additional solo albums in the Top-5.

▶ CHAPTER 12
THE RETURN OF THE WILBURYS

A couple months before the four members of the Traveling Wilburys had regrouped for their second effort, Bob Dylan and George Harrison would work together on Dylan's 1990 album, *Under The Red Sky*. Harrison provided a slide guitar solo on the album's title track.

Veteran producer Don Was recalled the unorthodox session: "There was a deep and long-standing friendship between George and Bob, and the mood was quite jocular. Before George had even heard the song, Bob sat in the engineer's seat, hit 'record,' and said, 'Play!' Apparently, it was not the first time he'd done this to George. It was a respectable solo, but way out of tune – well, George didn't even know what key the song was in! Bob indicated that the solo was perfect and that we were done. George rolled his eyes, turned to me and asked, 'What do you think, Don?' Suddenly, all the oxygen was sucked out of the room. The [man who oversaw the] Concert For Bangladesh was sitting two feet away awaiting words of wisdom! How am I gonna tell George Harrison his solo wasn't up to snuff? What if Bob really did think it was a good solo? I decided I wasn't hired to be their adoring fan. 'It was really good. But let's see if you can do an even better one,' I said. '*Thank you*,' answered George. Bob laughed, rewound the tape." Harrison was flawless on the second take, which was the version that appeared on the album.

During this period, Dylan also made a guest appearance at a concert by Tom Petty and the Heartbreakers at the Los Angeles Forum. After a solo performance of "Rainy Day Women #12 & 35," Dylan was joined by Petty for a rendition of an obscure 1950s rockabilly song by Glen Glenn, "Everybody's Movin'."

In the press, Del Shannon and Roger McGuinn were both mentioned as possible replacements for Roy Orbison in the Traveling Wilburys. Even Eric Clapton's name came up in the rumor mills. *Spy* magazine humorously offered ten potential replacements including Barry White, arguing that the deep-voiced R&B singer "would do double duty as the Wilbury of Love." During a television interview, George Harrison said that both Jerry Lee Lewis or Little Richard could be Wilburys, but not George Michael or Hall & Oates.

Although Tom Petty would refute the rumors, Harrison was more open-minded about adding another member to the group: "You can't replace Roy Orbison.... It's not every day you form a group with all these legends. That's not to say there aren't other Wilburys floating around out there. But the four of us need to talk, really, and keep an openness about it."

McGuinn, a co-founder of the Byrds, later recalled an incident in 1990, during the period when the Traveling Wilburys were recording their second album: "I was in L.A. busy building the tracks for my *Back From Rio* album. George invited me to come and live at the house where they were all recording, it was around the corner: 'Come on over and hang out!' I said, 'I really can't. Because I'm so busy with this pre-production for *Back From Rio*.' So that was that. You can draw your own conclusions what might have happened." (Later, after finishing the Wilburys sessions, Petty would co-write and share co-lead vocal duties with McGuinn on *Back From Rio's* first single, "King Of The Hill.")

Del Shannon had first met George Harrison and the rest of the Fab Four when the two acts shared an all-star bill at the Royal Albert Hall in London. It was during this period that Shannon mistakenly believed that he had received permission to record the Lennon-McCartney composition, "From Me To You," which at the time was at Number One in the U.K., but completely unknown in the U.S. Then in June 1963, Shannon's record label released his version of the song in the U.S., which managed to hit *Billboard's* Hot-100, but not the Top-40. Nonetheless, it became the first Lennon-McCartney composition to chart in the U.S.

Meanwhile, Jeff Lynne was particularly fond of Shannon

and often called him his first musical hero. In 1962, a 14-year-old Lynne saw his first-ever rock concert at the Town Hall in Birmingham, England, which was headlined by Shannon and also featured Dion, Joe Brown and Buzz Clifford. Lynne explained: "I think the first records that inspired me to want to do music were Del Shannon's. I also loved Roy Orbison, for a different reason. I think some of Orbison's recordings are still among the best pop records ever made."

Lynne first met Shannon nearly a decade later: "I met him in 1971, in a club in Birmingham (England) called Barbarella's. We sat and talked for about an hour, and I thought he was the funniest bloke. Little did I know that he'd always got a bottle of vodka stuck down his overcoat. I didn't realize he was drunk. But he was the nicest person that was drunk that I've ever known. Just wonderful. He came to my house in Birmingham and we jammed in my front room. When ELO used to come tour in America, he'd invite me to his house in the [Los Angeles] Valley."

Beginning in December 1973 and continuing into the following year, Lynne had the opportunity to work with his musical idol. Visiting Shannon's home in California, Lynne and a few other members of ELO worked on several tracks at Cherokee Studios in Hollywood, including "Distant Ghost," which was released a decade later. Another track, "Raylene," was co-written by Lynne and Shannon and had a strong ELO influence.

With his career on the decline, Shannon battled alcoholism for years. In the late-1970s, he began working on new tracks. A subsequent album, *Drop Down And Get Me*, was produced by

Petty and featured the Heartbreakers on a number of tracks. Although the album was not a strong seller, Shannon's remake of the rock oldie "Sea Of Love" reached the top-40 charts in 1982. By the late 1980s, both Lynne and Petty would again work with Shannon, this time together on the album, *Rock On!* As a favor to Shannon, Petty and Lynne had written one of the tracks, "Walk Away." But tragically, Shannon would not live to complete the album. The posthumously released project was completed by Petty, Lynne and Mike Campbell.

The sudden death of Del Shannon on February 8, 1990, put an end to the speculation that he might replace Orbison in the Wilburys. The 55-year-old rocker, who had been battling a severe bout of depression, shot himself with a rifle. However, with the singer failing to leave behind a suicide note, his widow initially thought the shooting was accidental. Later, she blamed his actions on the side effects of the medication he was taking, Prozac, and filed a highly-publicized lawsuit against the drug's maker.

▶ CHAPTER 13
RECORDING THE SECOND ALBUM

In February 1990, the first Traveling Wilburys album won a Grammy for Best Rock Performance by a Duo or Group with Vocal, but would lose to Bonnie Raitt in the category of Album of the Year. In the end, *The Traveling Wilburys, Vol. 1* would sell three-million copies in the U.S.

The sessions for the second Traveling Wilburys album began in the spring of 1990. For the project, the members of the group gave themselves a new batch of nicknames: Boo Wilbury (Dylan), Clayton Wilbury (Lynne), Muddy Wilbury (Petty) and Spike Wilbury (Harrison).

Although Harrison was in charge during the making of the first album, this time around Dylan took the reins and also provided more of the vocals. As a gag, the second album was titled, *The Traveling Wilburys, Vol. 3*. Lynne recalled, "That was George's idea.... He said, 'Let's confuse the buggers.'" Not surprisingly, *Vol. 3* was dedicated to Lefty Wilbury (Orbison).

After determining which weeks all four members would be

free from commitments, they agreed to meet in late April. Dylan had the tightest schedule and was forced to fit the sessions in between two tours.

The surviving four Wilburys decided to splurge on the sessions by leasing a furnished, 1920s, Spanish-style, hilltop mansion. As longtime Dylan confidant Victor Maymudes remembered: "For the second album they rented a German's castle in Hollywood, which was unbelievable. The only stipulation was they couldn't film or take pictures of the paintings on the wall. It felt like the owner was insinuating that nobody should know the paintings were even on that wall. Huge works of art, thirty-foot paintings and tapestries." The grounds of the estate featured lush flower gardens and an exquisite stone patio that offered a respite between takes.

At one point, a towering Wilbury flag – featuring the group's logo – was hoisted above the compound, which was nicknamed both Camp Wilbury and Wilbury Mountain Studio. During much of the sessions, Harrison's son Dhani – who brought along his skateboard – and Dylan's son Jakob were in a second-floor bedroom playing video games.

The album was recorded in the mansion's library, with the four members of the group sitting in a semi-circle on folding metal chairs. The drums were set up, about ten feet away, in an adjacent hallway. Much of the recording equipment – which was crammed against one side of the library – was loaned to the band by A&M Records.

Preferring to record in an informal setting, Petty explained: "People don't listen to records in a room that's all soundproofed and baffled up and set up for stereo dynamics. So if you can make one in a house, it's a luxury. And you don't have to walk past a receptionist." The library was dotted with a number of comfortable sofas and reading chairs, and was illuminated by ambient table lamps. The wooden bookshelves were accentuated by volumes of classic books. On the walls were a number of small oil portraits.

The four men quickly jumped into the process of writing and recording, with no preconceptions about the direction of the project. And just like the sessions for the first album, Lynne showed up wearing a Tom Petty t-shirt.

Dylan handled the responsibility of writing most of the lyrics. As Lynne explained at the time: "We all throw in ideas and words. But when you've got a lyricist like Bob Dylan – well, what are you gonna do?"

Lynne recounted the recording process: "We just set up in the library, the four of us with acoustic guitars and Jim Keltner on drums, and we just started writing songs. We actually sit down and do them right on the spot. We got the first songs going in half an hour, and we started recording it in probably an hour. One take and it's done. Then we start another one. If we get stuck, there's always somebody who'll go, 'Well, hang on, if we can't get out of that, let's go over here, let's try this chord.' Sometimes it's me who says that. Sometimes it's Tom, or Bob, or George. It's really like a co-op."

Petty and Dylan provided the lead vocals on most of the tracks. As such, Roy Orbison's absence was apparent. Dylan pondered at the time, "There's no telling what kind of record we could have made with Roy. Everyone missed him, but it wasn't like anyone sat around and talked about it." But drummer Jim Keltner noticed a difference in the tone of the sessions: "It was Roy's presence [that] made them rise to the occasion. The second album was really deflated... it was just sad and the enthusiasm wasn't there. So the writing suffered."

However, there was another difference between the two sessions. Dylan told an interviewer at the time, "Last time, it was a pretty rushed affair. A lot of stuff was just scraped up from jam tapes. This time, there was a whole lot left over. The songs are more developed. If people liked the first one, they'll love this one." A number of guests showed up during the sessions including Warner Brothers executives Mo Ostin and Lenny Waronker.

Just like the first album, the second set was written, recorded and mixed in about six weeks, with the project completed at Harrison's home studio. Also like the first album, *Vol. 3* was engineered by Richard Dodd.

But not all was well on the homefront for two of the Wilburys: while Petty had just reconciled with his wife after a painful separation, Dylan would soon be served with dissolution papers from his wife of four years.

The Traveling Wilburys, Vol. 3 was released on October 6 – just two weeks before Petty would turn 40. This time around, Warner Brothers spent some advertising dollars on a television commercial and print ads.

Rock critic Jon Pareles of *The New York Times* said of the album: "[it] stays close to 1950's and early 1960's rock roots, drawing on blues, doo-wop, rockabilly and Buddy Holly. But it is faster, jokier, lighter and meaner than the first album, as the band indulges its bile and paranoia along with humor." But

96

Rolling Stone magazine gave the album just three-and-a-half stars. In a review, rock critic Don McLeese wrote: "Inevitably, the album lacks the element of surprise that made *Vol. 1* such a fresh pleasure, and the soaring strains of the late, irreplaceable Roy Orbison are missed."

Not as successful as the debut Wilburys release, the second album did not contain any breakout hits. The project's most enduring tracks were "Inside Out" and "She's My Baby." While the album enjoyed heavy airplay on rock radio, top-40 stations ignored all of the tracks.

Harrison recalled: "The first song we wrote was called 'Inside Out.' From everybody arriving at the house, within an hour we had that song written. Not the lyrics, but we had the format for the tune. Then we put it down on tape – one take, two takes maybe." The song was released as a commercial single in Europe.

The album opened with the uptempo, "She's My Baby." All four members shared the lead vocal duties on the song. A strong rocker, it was far more guitar-oriented than anything on the group's first album. The track was not issued as a commercial single in the U.S.

For the British release of "She's My Baby," the B-side was a remake of the Del Shannon classic, "Runaway." The track featured Lynne on the clavioline, a vintage electronic keyboard which was a forerunner to the modern, analog synthesizer. Another track on the album, "The Devil's Been Busy," featured a rare sitar solo by Harrison.

The album's fan favorite, "Wilbury Twist," featured the guitarwork of former Thin Lizzy legend Gary Moore – who was given the nickname, Ken Wilbury. (For a time in the 1980s, Moore was close friends with Harrison and had turned down an offer to join Dylan's backing band.) In the song's music video, comedian John Candy demonstrated how to perform the newly-invented Wilbury Twist. A number of celebrities made cameo appearances in the video including Cheech Marin, Eric Idle, Whoopi Goldberg, Woody Harrelson, and even the lip-syncing duo Milli Vanilli. (Most of the cameos were missing from the 2007 DVD edition of the music video.)

It was ironic that the Wilburys would record a dance song considering the fact that none of the members were known for their dance moves except for Petty and Harrison, who on rare occasions would engage in some very brief, onstage, dance routines. However, in Harrison's music video for his solo hit "I Got My Mind Set On You," he chose to use a body double to perform a complex dance routine. (The late Roy Orbison would often perform entire concerts without stepping away from his microphone.)

In addition, the Wilburys also donated a track to the charity album, *Nobody's Child: The Romanian Angel Appeal.* The group recorded a version of "Nobody's Child," a folk song that Harrison first recorded in 1961 when the Beatles (billed as the Beat Brothers) had backed singer Tony Sheridan. ("Nobody's Child" was originally recorded in 1949 by American country singer Hank Snow, but Harrison was more familiar with a 1956 version by Scottish skiffle star Lonnie Donegan.) The Wilburys' version of the song featured Harrison on lead vocals, and included a newly written second verse.

As for touring in support of the second album, the group's

members remained elusive. When a Canadian interviewer posed the question to George Harrison, he stated, "We're going over Niagara Falls in a barrel of beer." The interviewer reminded Harrison that it would be his first real tour since 1974, but the former Beatle insisted that touring, night after night, "it's too tiring.... it's not my idea of fun."

Lynne later explained: "George had some wacky ideas about how the Wilburys could tour. His first was that we'll rent an aircraft carrier and then fly to different ports and let everyone climb onto the aircraft carrier and have a listen. His next idea was to tour by train. We'd pull into a station, drop a stage and play. But we never got around to either of them. Everyone had their own tours to do." Harrison was not particular fond of the grueling life on the road that a tour entails, nor the prospect of being confined inside a hotel room, in city after city.

Having never toured, the Traveling Wilburys remained a studio-only group. Ironically, Harrison was in the same situation two decades earlier, when as a member of the Beatles, he continued to release records but did not tour over a four-year span. Before breaking up in April 1970, the group had not appeared on a concert stage since August 29, 1966, when they performed for nearly 25,000 fans at Candlestick Park in San Francisco. (The group's only public performance during this period was an impromptu rooftop concert in 1969, which was stopped by police after a crowd had gathered on the streets below.) Similarly, Elvis Presley had continued to record albums and star in a series of Hollywood films, despite not appearing on a concert stage from 1961 until his triumphant *Comeback Special* in 1968.

▶ CHAPTER 14

ALL THINGS MUST PASS

After wrapping up the recording sessions for his final studio album at MCA Records, Tom Petty took his family to the quaint coastal town of St. Augustine, Florida, for the summer. The next Heartbreakers tour would not begin until the last week of August. Staying at a beach house overlooking the Atlantic Ocean, Petty felt relaxed for the first time in years.

Released in July 1991, *Into The Great Wide Open* displayed a mature sound. The group's first album in four years, the project was mostly produced by Jeff Lynne. But Lynne's production style was foreign to most of the Heartbreakers. Unlike previous recording sessions in which the entire group would be present at the sessions, Lynne preferred to record each musician, individually, one track at a time. Petty defended Lynne's production technique: "I think it was probably the only time he worked with a band... Dealing with the politics of a band just drives him nuts. It can drive anyone nuts – and especially [the Heartbreakers]. I think they were a little indignant I'd done a solo album." But as seasoned professionals, the members of the Heartbreakers eventually adjusted to Lynne's recording method. Petty recalled: "They dug Jeff. It was a good vibe, you know, having a new person in the room. We all tended to listen to him more than we would each other. He's very cheerful at sessions.... And he has a real good sense of organization, so he gets a lot done each day."

However, music writer Bill Flanagan argued that the album was radically different from the group's previous efforts: "Maybe it was a case of too many cooks, maybe it was the awkwardness of the Heartbreakers trying to fit Lynne's blueprint but the spontaneity that had marked all of Petty's projects since *Let Me Up* was missing. *Into The Great Wide Open* had some terrific individual tracks, and produced some hit singles, but overall the album felt labored-over in a way Petty's other recent work had not." Another critic was far less charitable, describing the album as "full of hazy references, half-baked concepts, unresolved tales, cliched metaphors and strained poetic meaning."

The subdued track, "Learning To Fly," was an unusual choice as the album's debut single. Composed by Petty and Lynne, the song was based on a military pilot's interview during the Gulf War and typified Petty's knack for ambiguous imagery. The song's music video was directed by Julien Temple and filmed at Bob's Airpark, a surreal airplane graveyard in Tucson, Arizona.

Meanwhile, George Harrison hesitantly returned to the stage in 1991, but only on a limited basis. It would be Harrison's first tour in 17 years. Harrison had not forgotten how poorly his 1974 North American tour had been received by both the press and fans alike, due to his reluctance to perform more than four Beatles songs and particularly because of his dry, gravelly vocals at many of the shows. Promoted as "the Dark Horse" tour, it was derided by some as "the Dark Hoarse" tour.

Although he had nixed a Traveling Wilburys tour, Harrison was convinced by Eric Clapton to hit the road for a 13-date tour. Several years earlier in 1985, Harrison and Clapton were part of a band that had backed rockabilly legend Carl Perkins at the tribute concert, *Blue Suede Shoes: A Rockabilly Session.* Another musician at the concert observed, "[Eric] and George were pals, you could tell."

The chief reason that Harrison had agreed to tour with Clapton was to help his longtime friend grieve over the loss of his young son, Conor, who had been killed earlier that year after falling from an open window.

Harrison and Clapton maintained a very non-traditional relationship, and managed to stay friends despite the fact that Clapton had previously courted Harrison's first wife, Pattie Boyd, who was the subject of the Derek and the Dominoes hit, "Layla." Harrison felt that his occupation encouraged such indiscretions, and he could not hold a grudge against a fellow musician.

During the tour, Harrison was backed by Clapton and his

band for a series of dates across Japan. Wanting to avoid a repeat of his 1974 tour, Harrison temporarily gave up smoking to protect his voice.

Across Japan, Harrison was amused by chants of "Georgie" from the appreciative audiences. Surprisingly, the concerts did not feature any Traveling Wilburys songs. Also, Harrison generally plodded along when singing his Fab Four classics such as "Something" and "Taxman."

Although various media sources claimed there was some onstage friction between Harrison and Clapton, Harrison later denied the reports. After the completion of the tour in December 1991, Harrison contemplated playing shows in Europe and the United States. That never came to fruition. Instead, an album from the tour was released in July 1992, *Live In Japan*. On the liner notes, Harrison was credited as Spike and Nelson Wilbury.

Harrison made a surprise announcement in 1992 and staged his first full-length concert in Britain since the breakup of the Beatles. On April 6, he performed at a fundraising show for the Natural Law Party of Britain. Opening the concert were Joe Walsh and Gary Moore. Hitting the Royal Albert Hall stage, Harrison began his 16-song set with a 1966 Beatles track from *Revolver*, "I Want To Tell You," and closed with the Chuck Berry classic, "Roll Over Beethoven." Again, Harrison did not perform a single Wilburys track.

Also that year, Harrison made a surprise visit to a Tom Petty and the Heartbreakers concert in Germany. But when Petty invited him onstage, Harrison replied: "It's so loud and smokey, and they are acting so crazy. I just feel better back here."

✦ ✧ ✦ ✧ ✦

On October 16, 1992, a 30th anniversary tribute to Bob Dylan was staged at Madison Square Garden, marking the release of his first album, *Bob Dylan*, which sold a mere 2,500 copies in 1962. All of Dylan's surviving bandmates in the Traveling Wilburys performed at the concert – which the press dubbed "Bobfest." Also performing were a host of rock dignitaries including Roger McGuinn, Eric Clapton and Neil Young.

Introducing Dylan to the crowd, George Harrison referred to him by his Wilburys persona: "Some of you may call him Bobby. Some of you may call him Zimmy. I call him Lucky. Ladies and gentleman, please welcome Bob Dylan." The impeccably dressed Dylan took the stage and began his set with "Song To Woody," a tribute his musical idol, Woody Guthrie, and one of the very first songs penned by Dylan.

One of the evening's musical highlights came when Tom Petty and the Heartbreakers performed an upbeat rendition of the Dylan standard, "Rainy Day Women #12 & 35." Afterward, the Heartbreakers remained on the stage as Petty introduced McGuinn, who delivered an extended version of the Dylan composition, "Mr. Tambourine Man," which was a career-making hit for the Byrds in 1965.

But the night's most talked-about moment came when eccentric Irish singer Sinead O'Connor was booed off the stage. The audience was responding to her actions two weeks earlier during an appearance on *Saturday Night Live*, when she ripped a photograph of the pope and shouted, "fight the real enemy."

The tribute would mark the last-ever paid concert appearance by George Harrison. Not a fan of the stage, Harrison had rarely performed in public during the last two decades of his life.

In February 1994, Jeff Lynne experienced a highlight of his professional career when he was offered the opportunity to work with the three surviving Beatles. The Fab Four were assembling their *Anthology* album series and were looking to complete some demo tracks recorded in the 1970s by John Lennon. Yoko Ono had given the tapes to Paul McCartney when Lennon was inducted into the Rock and Roll Hall of Fame as a solo artist.

It was George Harrison who convinced his bandmates that they needed a producer, if for no other reason but to keep their individual egos in check. Lynne wasn't the only producer they considered, but in the end, he was the one they picked. Surprisingly, George Martin had not been selected to do the work.

Lynne was already friendly with the two of the Beatles, but he barely knew McCartney. As such, McCartney later admitted: "I was worried. He's such a pal of George's. They'd done the Wilburys, and I was expecting him to lead it that way. To tell you the truth, I thought that he and George might create a wedge, saying, 'We're doing it this way' and I'd be pushed out. But he was very fair, and very thorough. He looked at things with a fine-tooth comb – if you can 'look' at things with a fine-tooth comb. He was very precise."

Lynne oversaw the sessions for two *new* Beatles tracks, "Free As A Bird" and "Real Love." A master producer who was accustomed to piecing together individual voices and instruments, and recording one musician or vocalist at a time, Lynne was the perfect choice for the project.

Lynne recalled: "They spent the first day reminiscing, just George, Paul and Ringo and me, sitting around the table having a laugh, telling stories about the old days. Which I can never repeat, of course. Some of them were rude ones. Just to be there for that was good enough. The other bit was a bit scarier. Actually making a record out of a cassette with John [Lennon's] voice and piano stuck together in mono. I did it at two or three in the morning because I didn't want to mess it up and have them go, 'Ha ha! You can't do it!' The next day Paul comes bounding out and says, 'You've done it! Well done!,' and gave me a great big hug. It was the best thing that could ever happen." (Lynne and the three surviving Beatles had also worked on a third track, the ballad "Now And Then," but Harrison vetoed its release.)

Meanwhile, the trio of Harrison, Lynne and Petty remained close friends, and would meet every few months just to socialize and catch up on things. During these visits, the subject of reforming the Wilburys was frequently discussed. Although all three men wanted to reform the group and record a third album, they never got around to scheduling the sessions. Dylan, meanwhile, maintained a heavy touring schedule and rarely joined these get-togethers.

◆ ◇ ◆ ◇ ◆

By the mid-1990s, George Harrison again retreated from his music career and public life, and went back to the daily routine of tending to the extensive gardens at his large English estate. As his wife Olivia explained, he would say: "I've just let go of all of that. I don't care about records, about films, about being on television or all that stuff." Although Harrison continued to write music and record in his home studio, little of his work would ever be released.

In July 1997, Harrison made a surprise appearance on VH1 as a favor to Ravi Shankar, who was promoting a new album. During the hour-long interview, Harrison was handed a guitar and agreed to perform some music. Casually dressed and sporting a greying beard, he played acoustic versions of several songs including "All Things Must Pass" and a Traveling Wilburys track from *Vol. 3*, "If You Belonged To Me." This would mark Harrison's final television appearance.

Also in 1997, two of the Wilburys experienced major health issues. In May, Bob Dylan nearly died after suffering a viral infection of the lining of his heart. Meanwhile, Harrison was diagnosed with throat cancer and later had surgery to remove a small portion of his lung. But while battling the disease, Harrison suffered a setback. At 3:30 in the morning on December 30, 1999, someone broke into Harrison's Friar Park estate. Shouting and making irrational accusations, the 33-year-old mentally unstable man from Liverpool ran upstairs to confront Harrison. After the two men began brawling, the intruder jumped on top of the former Beatle, stabbing him numerous times. The attacker was eventually subdued with aid of Harrison's wife, Olivia, who repeatedly struck the man with both a lamp and fireplace poker.

Charlie Watts of the Rolling Stones later revealed the details of the attack: "I spoke to Ringo about a month after it happened and he told me exactly what went on, and it was horrific. George was stabbed about 40 times. It happened outside his bedroom on the landing. He would have been dead if he'd been lying in bed, he wouldn't have been able to fight. The papers did say that one wound punctured his lung, but a lot of the others were just as horrific. The man was slashing him everywhere. George's wife hit him again and again on the head with this brass lamp, but he just wouldn't stop. There was blood everywhere." Later asked about the break-in, Harrison joked: "The man certainly wasn't auditioning for the Traveling Wilburys." Meanwhile, a relieved Tom Petty reportedly sent a short note to Harrison that read, "Aren't you glad you married a Mexican woman?"

While Harrison would eventually recover from the stab wounds, the added strain to his system would ultimately be too much for him to overcome. Although the cancer was declared cured by 1998, it would return the following year and spread to his brain. On November 29, 2001, Harrison passed away at Paul McCartney's home in Los Angeles. He was just 58. According to Olivia Harrison, the room lit up at the moment of her husband's death.

Lynne had spent much time with Harrison in his final days, and softly played Harrison's favorite instrument – a ukelele – by his bedside. The death of his close friend hit Petty especially hard at a time when he was battling a number of personal demons. Petty later said of Harrison, "I was mostly just amazed that he would take the time to sit down and play guitar with me. The first time we played together.... it struck me that here's this guy who is a hero of mine, but he's also just a guy who loves the guitar as much as I do. George was a very gracious person, and he always brought little gifts – like hats and Beatles watches – when he came to visit. I loved his humor. I remember telling him once how much I admired his sound with the Beatles, and he said, 'Oh, we had those Gretsches. If only we'd had Strats, we could have been really good!'"

But Petty was also hoping to record another Traveling Wilburys album: "We never thought we were gonna run out of time." Petty later recalled: "My daughter Adria used to visit him a lot in England when she was over there. She would go and stay at Friar Park. She was telling me the other [day] that one night they were out walking in the garden and he goes, 'Oh, Adria, I just wish I could turn into a light beam and go away.'"

Harrison's remains were flown to London, where wife Olivia and son Dhani were joined by two Hare Krishna devotees who performed Hindu rites. Harrison's ashes were later immersed in the Ganges River in the town of Varanasi, India, with his family requesting a worldwide minute of meditation. Both Lynne and Petty remained close to Dhani and assumed some fatherly duties.

Staged at the prestigious Royal Albert Hall in London, the Concert for George was a musical tribute to the fallen Beatle on the one-year anniversary of his death. Harrison's longtime friend Eric Clapton recalled: "In the spring of 2002, Brian [Roylance] came around for dinner and we started talking about George.... I ventured to remark that it was sad that there would be no memorial for George, at least in a music sense, and Brian said, 'Not unless you do something.' So that trap was sprung, and I happily walked into it. The program was a labor of love in which I threw myself. Over the next few months, Olivia [Harrison] and Brian and I planned the event, discussing who we would ask and what songs we would play. Olivia was the mastermind of the whole thing, and I simply assembled the rock part of the musical end.... The only minor difficulty arose over who should sing 'Something.'"

Tickets to the tribute concert quickly sold out, despite the nearly $250 admission charge. All of the proceeds were donated to a charity founded by Harrison in 1973, the Material World Charitable Foundation.

On the evening of November 29, 2002, the Concert for George opened with Eric Clapton offering a few words to the audience. He then introduced the evening's first musical act, the legendary sitar player Ravi Shankar and his daughter Anoushka. (Harrison had first traveled to India in 1966 to study with Ravi Shankar.)

The house band included Paul McCartney and Ringo Starr. While the back of the stage was graced by a large framed monitor that displayed a series of Harrison portraits, the front of the stage was rimmed with hundreds of flower bouquets brought by fans.

Early in the show, Jeff Lynne performed "I Want To Tell You" and "Give Me Love," and was joined by Eric Clapton on "If I Needed Someone." At one point, Clapton stated: "A lot of grief's been dealt with by playing this music."

Dressed in dark suits, Tom Petty and the Heartbreakers later performed a pair of Beatles-era songs composed by Harrison, "Taxman" and "I Need You." The group was then joined on the stage by Lynne and Harrison's son, Dhani, for an upbeat rendition of "Handle With Care," which was the best-received performance of Petty's short set. Petty and Lynne seemed genuinely elated to be on the stage, celebrating their close friend's legacy. (Petty had originally wanted to perform Harrison's favorite Wilburys track, "If You Belonged To Me.") Petty recounted: "In the afternoon, Dhani came up to me and asked if he could join in on the Wilburys song. When we played it, it really felt like George was on the stage."

Lynne remained on stage, playing an acoustic guitar, as Billy Preston and Eric Clapton led an emotional rendition of "Isn't It A Pity," a song written by Harrison in 1966 that appeared on his 1970 solo album, *All Things Must Pass*. (The song had been rejected by the other members of the Beatles.)

The concert ended with Joe Brown playing the ukulele on a touching performance of the pop standard, "I'll See You In My Dreams." Brown, one of Britain's first rockers, had toured on the same bill as the Beatles in 1962. Later, Brown served as the best man when Harrison married Olivia Arias in 1978.

Many in attendance were curious about Bob Dylan's absence. Although Dylan was originally slated to appear, his name was removed from the lineup without explanation. Dylan was touring at the time and referenced the event while on stage in Virginia, where he performed the Harrison chestnut, "Something." Also missing from the tribute were Yoko Ono, Julian Lennon, Sean Lennon and Harrison's frequent collaborator, Gary Wright.

In the late-1990s, George Harrison had been working on new tracks for a planned solo album, which was titled *Brainwashed*. Then, four months after Harrison's death 2001, Jeff Lynne received a box containing the unfinished tracks. The songs had been recorded on traditional analogue audiotapes. Lynne recalled: "It wasn't the first time I'd heard these songs. George had played them all for me live on his ukelele. I knew he'd been working on them in the studio, and we'd been talking about producing them together when we found the time.... He knew he wasn't going to be able to finish [the album], and before he died he asked me to do it for him. His only advice was, 'Don't make it too posh!'"

The album was completed over a six-month period, the following year, by Lynne and Harrison's son, Dhani. As a tribute to Harrison, Lynne managed to sneak in a ukelele on every track. Lynne recalled: "It was so depressing, as I couldn't turn around and say, 'What do you think of that?' George wasn't there to answer for himself." But Dhani Harrison insisted at the time: "I've been a real control freak about this project and rightly so. Some people would have wanted to make this album all sad and depressing. It's not supposed to feel that way. It's not meant to mop up loose ends. My dad never felt sorry for himself. He was a very strong man with a great sense of humor."

Released in November 2002, *Brainwashed* was certified Gold in the U.S. for sales of more than 500,000 copies. One reviewer said of the project: "Much of the material deals with big issues – the unending cycle of nature, the eternal mystery of our purpose in the universe, the essence of love – there is no depression here, no regret, no bitterness or complaint."

Another critic wrote, *"Brainwashed* starts with a jaunty, Traveling Wilburys-soundalike, 'Any Road.'" Released as a single, the track was a minor hit in the U.K. Another song, "Run So Far," was first recorded by Eric Clapton on his *Journeyman* album in 1989, with Harrison on guitar. The album's liner notes featured a quotation by the Bhagavad Gita: "There never was a time when you or I did not exist. Nor will there be any future when we shall cease to be."

In 2002, Harrison scored a surprise number-one single in both the U.K. and Canada when "My Sweet Lord" was re-released. Lost in history is the fact that Harrison had originally recorded the song in 1970 with Billy Preston on lead vocals.

In late-2005, Olivia Harrison asked Tom Petty and Jeff Lynne to be the presenters for Harrison's solo induction into the Rock and Roll Hall of Fame, the following spring. Although Petty was quick to oblige, Lynne had to be persuaded due to his disdain for public appearances.

With "Wilbury Twist" playing in the background, Petty and Lynne took the stage at the Waldorf Astoria in New York City.

Standing at the podium, Petty offered a tribute to Harrison: "He just loved playing music with his friends. And he loved guitars. And he loved rock and roll. And he loved Carl Perkins. And he loved Little Richard. And he loved Dhani and Olivia. And he loved to stay up all night long and play the ukulele till dawn." While Petty's poignant speech lasted just a little over four minutes – which was very brief by Rock Hall standards – the somewhat reclusive Lynne followed Petty with just a 20-second statement. Olivia Harrison's selection of Petty and Lynne – instead of the two surviving Beatles – was a surprise to many and demonstrated the close friendship that Petty and Lynne had cultivated with the former Beatle. (Much like the situation at the Concert for George tribute in 2002, many of the attendees at the Rock Hall induction lamented the absence of Bob Dylan.)

Later that evening, Petty and Lynne performed two songs with an all-star band that included Steve Winwood, Jim Capaldi, Prince and George Harrison's 26-year-old son, Dhani, who looked far younger than his actual age. After a faithful rendition of "Handle With Care," the highlight of the evening came when Prince delivered a blistering guitar solo during an extended rendition of "While My Guitar Gently Weeps."

Shortly after Harrison's passing, singer Paul Simon reminisced about a visit to Friar Park, "The rhythm of the wind in the leaves and the cluster of chords of autumn's orange, gold and evergreen made it easy to understand why he'd chosen to spend the last thirty years gradually planting, pruning, editing and reshaping the land while at the time recasting himself from pop-culture icon to master gardener."

▶ CHAPTER 15
AFTER THE WILBURYS

The Traveling Wilburys remain a cherished part of rock lore. The gathering of five elder statesmen of rock offered a lesson – some supergroups really can succeed, make great music and sell lots of records. They would record just two albums and release only 25 songs.

In its list of the Best Albums of the 1980s, *Rolling Stone* placed *The Traveling Wilburys, Vol. 1* at #70, with the magazine explaining: "The Traveling Wilburys' album was one of those happy accidents waiting to happen.... The five half-brothers of the Wilbury family were hokey but hip, and their individual strengths complimented one anther perfectly." Petty's solo effort *Full Moon Fever*, which was the best-selling album of his career, came in at #92. None of his Wilburys bandmates placed an album on the list.

When Harrison's distribution deal with Warner Brothers expired in 1995 without being renewed, both of the Traveling Wilburys albums remained out-of-print for more than a decade.

Petty later explained, "George really wanted to do another Wilburys record, with the idea of bringing them all out on CD at once." Unfortunately, that never happened.

Finally, in 2007, the box set, *The Traveling Wilburys Collection*, was belatedly released by Rhino. The project topped the charts in several regions including Australia and the United Kingdom, and reached the top-10 in the U.S.

The box set included the group's two albums as well as two bonus tracks – "Maxine" and "Like A Ship" – which were unreleased outtakes from the *Vol. 3* sessions. Lynne explained at the time, "They were completed, except for some harmonies, so I asked George's son, Dhani, to do his father's parts, which was nice." Dhani Harrison was credited on the project as Ayrton Wilbury, which was intended as a tribute to Brazilian race driver Ayrton Senna. The track also featured a new guitar solo by Lynne. A similar treatment was given to the track, "Like A Ship." The box set also contained a short, lighthearted documentary, *The True History of the Traveling Wilburys*. Most of the footage was shot by Harrison during the sessions for the first album, using a portable handheld camera. A few of the scenes were filmed by drummer Jim Keltner and roadie Alan "Bugs" Weidel.

Individually, the members of the Traveling Wilburys had varying degrees of success in their post-supergroup careers. Some of them preferred to remain active, while others wanted solitude and privacy.

Of all the Wilburys, Tom Petty would have the most success in the 1990s and into the next decade. In December 2005, Tom Petty was awarded *Billboard* magazine's prestigious Century Award.

Just thirteen years earlier in 1992, Petty presented the inaugural award to George Harrison. At the podium, Petty delivered a quirky and touching address: "George Harrison makes me think of the fabulous Beatles arriving like a vision to an entire generation, of girls screaming, music better than you can dream of coming out of every radio. He makes me think of rockabilly solos and Gretsch guitars and Carl Perkins and Beethoven rolling over." In Harrison's acceptance speech, he described the Traveling Wilburys as "the band that made me remember how much fun it was to play rock and roll."

The day after George Harrison's posthumous induction into the Rock and Roll Hall of Fame in 2006, Petty and Lynne found themselves planning another musical collaboration. Petty recalled, "The performance went well, so on the trip back I said to [Lynne], 'We ought to do a track sometime.' Then, Mike [Campbell] and I went over to Jeff's house, showed him a tune, and he wanted to cut it right there in his studio. We didn't have a band, so Jeff said, 'You play drums don't you?' So I wound up being the drummer. Anyway, that first track went really nice, so we just pitched camp at Jeff's studio. I kept dragging out songs, and the next thing we knew, we'd recorded ten tracks. It was just the three of us. Jeff played bass, Mike played all the solos, and each one of us would fill in wherever we could on keyboard and guitar."

While recording the album, Petty began to ponder his legacy:

"Lately I've been concerned with what I'll leave behind artistically. The biggest priority with the new record now is that I know this is here longer than me and that's more important than [it] being a hit record. Years ago you'd have to make sure you had one [track] that was a [hit] single. I don't think that pops up in my mind anymore." More importantly, the album reflected Petty's personal serenity at the time: "It wouldn't have been a very good record if I just sat back and wrote about how happy I was. But I am pretty happy these days. I've gone through the dark tunnel and come out the other end.... I have a good family, my kids are doing well, and I have a young boy who just turned thirteen, and that's a whole movie on its own. I never really had any real family. My mom died when I was quite young, and my dad was never around much. And so when I married Dana, she and her mom and her brother lived down here, and they kind of adopted me into their family.... So I feel good having that kind of bond with a family."

Released in July 2006, *Highway Companion* was considered Petty's third solo album. Co-produced with Lynne and Campbell, the album received only moderate radio airplay. The track "Saving Grace" (not the 1980 Dylan song of the same name) was a retro-sounding, blues-inspired tune that was an unlikely choice as the album's lead radio single.

Also in 2006, four years after Tom Petty was inducted into the Rock and Roll Hall of Fame, the group was the subject of an exhibit at the lakefront museum in Cleveland. Most of the artifacts came from a storage closet at Petty's home in Malibu. "We left his house pinching ourselves," recalled Rock Hall curator Howard Kramer.

The Petty exhibit featured historic memorabilia such as one of the large, red velvet hats he wore in the Alice in Wonderland-inspired music video for "Don't Come Around Here No More;" the first version of the *Full Moon Fever* album cover, which was originally titled *Songs From The Garage*; and the grey jacket he wore while recording the first Traveling Wilburys album. (The following year, Orbison was the subject of his own exhibit at the museum.)

Petty went on to perform at the Super Bowl halftime show in 2010 – the only Wilbury invited to do so. Then in 2014, Petty scored the first-ever number-one album in his career with the blues-rock project, *Mojo*.

On his SiriusXM radio program, *Buried Treasure*, Petty would play his favorite Heartbreakers tunes as well tracks from his other groups, the Traveling Wilburys and Mudcrutch. Dylan, on the other hand, never played a single Wilburys track on his satellite radio show.

Petty continued to sell out large concert venues whenever he decided to tour. In time, Petty and the Heartbreakers would occasionally perform three Wilburys songs on stage: "Tweeter And The Monkey Man," "End Of The Line" and "Handle With Care" (with Scott Thurston singing Roy Orbison's vocal parts).

Meanwhile, in 1990, Jeff Lynne released his first solo album, *Armchair Theatre*. The project contained mostly original tracks as well as a song co-written with Tom Petty, "Blown Away," which featured backing vocals from Del

Shannon and some guitarwork from George Harrison.

Amazingly, *Armchair Theatre* stumbled on the charts and neither of the two singles – "Every Little Thing" and "Lift Me Up" – were more than minor hits. While Lynne had been able to weave his musical magic on albums for Tom Petty, Roy Orbison, George Harrison and the Traveling Wilburys, he fared poorly with his own solo venture. In fact, Lynne was the only member of the Traveling Wilburys who never managed to score a solo top-40 hit.

Lynne would move to the U.S. in 1997, purchasing a home in the Hollywood section of Los Angeles. He became the fourth Wilbury to make Los Angeles his home. Lynne had sold his home in England to Robin Campbell of UB40.

Following his work in 1995 with three surviving Beatles on the *Anthology* series, Lynne would go on to co-produce Paul McCartney's 1997 album *Flaming Pie* and three tracks for Ringo Starr's 2002 album *Time Takes Time*.

In 2012, Lynne released his second solo album, *Long Wave*. Recorded over a period of two years, it consisted of cover versions of songs which had influenced him early in his life. The project contained a straightforward version of the Roy Orbison classic, "Running Scared." But just like his previous effort, the album was not a strong seller.

Meanwhile, in 1986 when Lynne walked away from his other band, the Electric Light Orchestra, he was expecting to regroup after a short hiatus. But after enjoying a tremendous amount of success and personal satisfaction as a producer and member of the Traveling Wilburys, he saw no reason to rejoin his former bandmates in ELO. Lynne later explained: "I was a great collaborator, I discovered. It wasn't like I imagined. And of course *Full Moon Fever* was a big, big hit. That's still my favorite album that I've ever done."

After Lynne's former ELO bandmate Bev Bevan attempted to tour as ELO Part II, Lynne was forced to launch legal action on several occasions. Eventually, Bevan sold his rights to the ELO name to Lynne for an undisclosed sum.

In 2001, Lynne released the poor-selling ELO album, *Zoom*. More Beatlesque and ethereal than the group's previous albums, it did not spawn any radio hits. The project included only two classic members of ELO – Lynne and Richard Tandy – and featured guest appearances by George Harrison and Ringo Starr.

Although ELO was preparing to go on the road in support of the album, a scheduled 25-date tour across the U.S. and Canada was cancelled due to poor ticket sales. (The group had not performed in the U.S. since 1981, and had last performed in public in 1986.)

Instead, ELO would perform just two times during this period. Intended as warm-up shows in preparation for the tour, two performances were staged for a PBS television special at the CBS Television City studio in Los Angeles.

Lynne and ELO gave a pair of strong performances with a group that included his girlfriend at the time, Rosie Vela, on backing vocals. Lynne had first met a very nervous Vela when she was invited to perform for the Traveling Wilburys while they were recording their second album in 1990. A track from *Zoom*, "Stranger On A Quiet Street," was written by Lynne about the first time he met Vela.

Lynne received an unexpected honor in 2012. At the summer Olympics in London, Lynne's favorite ELO song, "Mr. Blue Sky," was played during both the opening and closing ceremonies.

At London's Hyde Park in 2014, Lynne staged his first full British concert in 30 years. Due to legal reasons, he was forced to adopt the moniker, Jeff Lynne's ELO. When asked about his absence from the road, Lynne responded: "Do I regret not touring more in the last 30 years? No, to be honest. I've had more fun in the studio. I've learnt a ton of stuff in that period."

At the concert, Lynne surprised the audience by performing "Handle With Care," which he dedicated to Roy Orbison and George Harrison. Lynne chose to sing all of the song's parts himself. In subsequent performances, his backing band assumed some of the vocal duties, with one member singing Orbison's part of the song and the others providing harmony.

In 2016, Jeff Lynne's ELO issued the album, *Alone In The Universe*. The project was recorded over an 18-month period at Lynne's expansive home studio, which he named Bungalow Palace. (Every room in his home was wired for recording.) Lynne admitted that he had Orbison in mind when he wrote and sang one of the album's tracks, "I'm Leaving You."

Of the five Wilburys, Lynne was the final member of the group to be inducted into the Rock and Roll Hall of Fame, when the Electric Light Orchestra was belatedly enshrined in 2017. The group was inducted by Dhani Harrison who told the audience that if his father was still alive, he would have been the one inducting the group. The younger Harrison recalled seeing his first-ever concert – a fundraiser starring ELO in 1986

– and his amazement at watching his own father perform for the first time: "My father gets up from his seat and tells me to wait for him.... He walked off and moments after he disappeared from view, suddenly he reappeared onstage carrying a guitar... Out of nowhere, in perfect unison, they all kicked into 'Johnny B. Goode.'"

Returning to his role as a producer, Lynne later worked with Ringo Starr's brother-in-law Joe Walsh on *Analog Man* and with Bryan Adams on the album, *Get Up*.

Late in his career, Lynne mused: "I've been incredibly lucky. I've worked with all the people I grew up loving, like the Beatles, Roy Orbison and Bob Dylan, and most of them have gone on to become friends as well. I've lived every fan's dream."

Following the untimely death of Roy Orbison, his wife and sons wanted to keep his music in the spotlight. In 1992, Jeff Lynne assembled an Orbison album from previously-released material as well as from demo sessions. The project, *King Of Hearts*, was a strong seller in the U.K. and spawned three British top-40 hits, including a re-released duet with k.d. lang, "Crying."

Then in 1998, Orbison's widow, Barbara, released *Combo Concert* on her own label, Orbison Records. The project consisted of previously unreleased live tracks from Holland and France, recorded in 1965. Also that year, she accepted an honor for her late husband, the Recording Academy's Lifetime

Achievement Award. Then, in 2010, Orbison received a star on the Hollywood Walk of Fame.

In 2011, Barbara Orbison died exactly 23 years to the day after the death of her husband. She succumbed to cancer. In 2016, Orbison's sons released the career-spanning anthology, *Roy Orbison: The Ultimate Collection.*

Musically, Orbison's torch was carried by singer-songwriter Chris Isaak, who enjoyed a career characterized by melancholy songs of heartache. Isaak once said of his musical mentor, "He had a great thing that he told me. 'People always think I have sad songs, but if you listen to my songs, I always put a little bit of hope in there.'" Isaak would eventually record a moody but faithful rendition of "Only The Lonely" and a track written but never recorded by Orbison, "So Long I'm Gone," which was originally covered by his Sun Records labelmate, Warren Smith. Isaak has performed a number of Orbison songs in concert, including "Leah" and "Oh, Pretty Woman." Then in 2004, Isaak was the natural choice to portray Orbison on the ABC television series, *American Dreams.* Then ten years later in 2014, Isaak was selected to induct Orbison into the Musicians Hall of Fame in Nashville.

Of all the Traveling Wilburys, Bob Dylan was the least likely to mention the band in interviews or to even acknowledge his membership in the supergroup. A performer with a musical repertoire that stretched into the hundreds and hundreds of his own compositions as well as countless rock and folk classics, somehow he has had trouble fitting a Wilburys track into his stage performances. So far, he has performed just one Wilburys track in concert, the bittersweet "Congratulations." Even in his 2004 autobiography, *Chronicles, Volume 1*, Dylan spent quite a bit of time talking about his tour with Tom Petty, but mentioned the Wilburys just one time and only in passing: "[In 1989] I had two records on the chart, even one in the top 10, *The Traveling Wilburys*. The other one was the *Dylan And The Dead* album."

Similarly, most Dylan biographies completely gloss over his membership in the group, as though his involvement in a fun, light-hearted ensemble – which avoided *serious* topics like protesting against corrupt government entities or the vagaries of organized religion – is somehow degrading to the reputation of the Voice of a Generation.

Shortly after completing the sessions for the first Traveling Wilburys album, Dylan launched his legendary Never Ending Tour. Maintaining a heavy touring schedule, he performed a minimum of seventy concerts a year – every year – for the next three decades.

During this period, Dylan also continued a heavy recording schedule. But unlike Petty, who also recorded on a regular basis, Dylan was unable to land any radio hits. In terms of recorded output, Dylan was the most prolific Wilbury, by far, releasing his 38th studio album in 2017. Remaining a musical chameleon, he shocked fans late in his career by recording an album of Frank Sinatra songs and then followed up with an album of pop standards such as "That Old Black Magic" and "It Had To Be You."

And although Dylan has released dozens of solo albums, he was the only Wilbury who never worked with Jeff Lynne as a producer. Their only collaboration came with an unreleased demo of "I'm In The Mood," which Lynne informally produced in Dylan's garage studio.

Additionally, Dylan was the only Wilbury to receive a Nobel Peace Prize. (In fact, he was the *only* rock singer, ever, to receive the award.) Honored in the field of literature, he was in no hurry to publically acknowledge the news and kept the Nobel Prize committee guessing as to whether or not he would even accept the award.

During his lifetime, Dylan was not the recipient of his fair share of honors, tributes or awards, and he did not earn his first Grammy until 1980, when the track, "Gotta Serve Somebody" was voted the Best Rock Vocal Performance by a Male. His groundbreaking, 1960s-era output – such as "Blowin' In The Wind," "Like A Rolling Stone" and "Mr. Tambourine Man" – were overlooked by the Grammy Awards. Consequently, winning a Grammy for his participation in the Traveling Wilburys was a genuine honor for Dylan.

What legacy did the Traveling Wilburys leave behind? In 2005, an *Entertainment Weekly* headline asked the question: What ever happened to the Traveling Wilburys? In the article, the magazine referred to the band as a "boomer-rock supergroup."

The surviving members of the Traveling Wilburys continued

to speculate about reuniting for an album or concert tour. In 2009, Petty admitted, "It's such a shame that everyone's not still here, because I still feel like I'm in that band." Then in 2015, Jeff Lynne pondered: "Could we do it again, start a new version of the Wilburys? Possibly, yes. I think if a couple of us wanted to do it, and the right people were interested, then it could work. But, you know, you couldn't ever recreate the experience. You could never capture the sheer enjoyment we all got from the Wilburys, the fun of it all, the freedom from pressure. Then there was the sheer surprise in what we did. Nobody expected it. If we were to do it again, I think we'd have to do something quite different musically." Had Roy Orbison not been struck down by a heart attack, he certainly would have pushed and prodded his bandmates to continue recording, as he certainly was the most enthusiastic member of the band.

Additionally, the decision by the Traveling Wilburys not to tour cost them plenty of radio airplay, album sales and media exposure as well the opportunity to connect with the group's fans. Had the Wilburys gone on the road – *traveling* and *twisting* down the rock and roll highway – the band would have certainly garnered a greater position in the pantheon of rock and roll royalty.

In 2017, two weeks before the annual induction ceremony, a writer at *The Cleveland Plain Dealer* posed the question in the headline: "Are the Traveling Wilburys Rock & Roll Hall of Fame Worthy?" In the piece, the writer noted that the "Traveling Wilburys are the only band to have every member inducted into the Rock Hall individually without the band being inducted." Another writer at the same newspaper echoed the sentiment: "Frankly, were it not for the deaths of Orbison and Harrison – Orbison of a heart attack at 52 in 1988 and Harrison of lung cancer at 58 in 2001 – I am convinced the Rock Hall would be inducting the Wilburys, too. The combination of voices, musicianship and especially songwriting in that group was nothing short of magical."

On October 1, 2017, Tom Petty suffered a massive heart attack at his home in Malibu. He was discovered unconscious on the floor by his wife. Rushed to UCLA Santa Monica Hospital, he passed away the following day. He was 66.

Traveling Wilburys bandmate Bob Dylan issued the statement: "It's shocking, crushing news. I thought the world of Tom. He was a great performer, full of the light, a friend, and I'll never forget him." Jeff Lynne added, "Tom Petty was the coolest guy I ever knew."

Just six days earlier, Petty had just finished the last show of a 44-date tour. Billed as the 40th Anniversary Tour, it was intended as Tom Petty and the Heartbreakers' final large-scale trek on the concert road. He closed out the tour with three triumphant shows at the Hollywood Bowl in Los Angeles.

In his final interview, Petty told a reporter: "This year has been a wonderful year for us. This has been that big slap on the back we never got.... It is grueling to do a very, very long [tour]. This was quite a long one. It's sometimes physically hard. But then the lights go down, you hear the crowd and you're all better. You feel like, 'OK, let's do it.'"

▶ EPILOGUE

When choosing a title for this book, we nearly called it, *The Traveling Wilburys: A Short History*. Why? The answer is simple: because the group was essentially a studio-only group. They were together for only two ten-day recording sessions and nothing more. As one of the editors remarked about the size of this book, "There's only so much you can say about the Traveling Wilburys."

We considered another title, *The Traveling Wilburys: A Complete History*, but somehow that didn't seem appropriate. There's something about this exceptional, all-star group that just doesn't seem complete, and there was definitely a need for some sort of closure. And, technically, the group never broke up. Tom Petty once stated that he reformed his pre-Heartbreakers group, Mudcrutch, because he "felt like there was some music there that got left behind." The same could be said about the Wilburys.

Instead, what remains of the Traveling Wiburys is a

mystique of unfulfilled possibilities and what could have been, much like a rock band that does not come out for an encore, even as the fans remain standing on their feet, clapping wildly and cheering at the top of their lungs.

► SELECTED BIBLIOGRAPHY

Atkins, Martyn (Director); & Pluta, James (Producer). (2014). *Mr. Blue Sky: The Story of Jeff Lynne & ELO*. Eagle Rock Entertainment.

Brown, Mick. (2007, September 8). *Stevie Nicks: A survivor's story. The (London) Telegraph*.

Cash, Johnny. (1997). *Cash: The Autobiography*. San Francisco: HarperSanFrancisco.

Clapton, Eric. (2007). *Clapton: The Autobiography*. New York: Broadway Books.

DeCurtis, Anthony. (1986, March 27). Dylan down under. *Rolling Stone*.

DeWitt, Howard A. (2001). *Stranger in Town: The Musical life of Del Shannon*. Dubuque, IA: Kendall/Hunt Publishing.

Dylan, Bob, (2004). *Chronicles: Volume One*. New York: Simon & Schuster.

Flanagan, Bill. (1986). *Written in My Soul*. Chicago: Contemporary Books.

Flanagan, Bill. (1986, April). Tom Petty pulls together: The Southern soul of a Hollywood rocker. *Musician*.

Freff. (1985, June). Tom Petty & Dave Stewart?! *Musician*.

Fricke, David. (2016, December 9). Interview. *Tom Petty Radio* (Sirius).

Fugelsang, John. (2001, November 29). *George Harrison: A Tribute*. VH-1.

George-Warren, Holly (Ed.). (2005). *Farm Aid: A Song for America*. New York: Rodale.

Goldberg, Danny. (2008). *Bumping into Geniuses*. New York: Gotham Books.

Goldberg, Michael. (1986, January 16). Back on the road. *Rolling Stone*.

Gundersen, Edna. (1990, February 9). Petty at his peak. *USA Today*.

Hiatt, Brian. (2011, September 15). The private life of George Harrison. *Rolling Stone*.

Hilburn, Robert. (1987, May 24). A Petty mood: A classic rocker's passion is refreshed. *The Los Angeles Times*.

Jones, Allan; & Love, Damien. (2014, August). What good am I? *Uncut*.

Leng, Simon. (2006). *While My Guitar Gently Weeps: The Music of George Harrison*. Milwaukee, WI: Hal Leonard.

Marks, Craig; & Tannenbaum, Rob. (2011). *I Want My MTV*. New York: Dutton.

McGee, Alan. (2008, October 16). "ELO: The band the Beatles could have been." *The Guardian*.

Moseley, Willie G. (2002, October). Chris Hillman: Bluegrass, bass, and back again. *Vintage Guitar*.

Petty, Tom. (2002, January 17). Remembering George. *Rolling Stone*.

Petty, Tom; & Lynne, Jeff. (2007). Promotional spot for *The Traveling Wilburys, Deluxe Edition*. Rhino.

Pond, Steve. (1989, January 26). Roy Orbison: 1936-1988. *Rolling Stone*.

Rosen, Craig. (2006, March 25). Tom Petty & The Heartbreakers. *Billboard*.

Rowan, Terry. (2015). *Penny Laine's Anthology*. Raleigh, NC: Lulu.

Rowland, Mark. (1990, March). The quiet Wilbury. *Musician*.

Schruers, Fred. (1999, July 7). Tom Petty: The *Rolling Stone* interview. *Rolling Stone*.

Scopa, Bud. (2007, September). The inside story of the Traveling Wilburys: Rock's greatest ever supergroup. *Uncut*.

Shelton, Robert. (2011). *No Direction Home: The Life and Music of Bob Dylan*. Milwaukee: Hal Leonard Corporation.

Smith, Joe. (1988). *Off the Record: An Oral History of Popular Music*. New York: Warner Books.

Sounes, Howard. (2001). *Down the Highway: The Life of Bob Dylan*. New York: Grove Press.

Stewart, Dave. (2008). *The Dave Stewart Songbook: The Stories Behind the Songs, Volume One*. Encinitas, CA: Surfdog.

Udovitch, Mim; & Wild, David. (2002, January 17). Remembering George. *Rolling Stone*.

Whitburn, Joel. (2008). *Rock Tracks 1981-2008*. Menomonee Falls, WI: Record Research.

Whitburn, Joel. (2009). *Top Pop Singles 1955-2008*. Menomonee Falls, WI: Record Research.

▶ NOTES

INTRODUCTION:
1. "Supergroups are almost always a..." ~ Milward, John. (1989, May 4). Petty and the Wilburys: Supergroup success story. *The Philadelphia Inquirer.*
2. "Just getting some famous people..." ~ Rowland, Mark. (1990, March). The quiet Wilbury. *Musician.*
3. "The effortless camaraderie amongst titans..." ~ Beviglia, Jim. (2015, October 18). Lyric of the week: Traveling Wilburys, "Not Alone Anymore. *American Songwriter.*
4. "We definitely didn't want to..." ~ Bauder, David. (1988, December 14). Legends joined to become "Traveling Wilburys." *The Fort Scott (Kansas) Tribune.*

CHAPTER 1: DYLAN & PETTY:
1. "Paul didn't ask me to..." ~ Jones, Dylan. (2013). *The Eighties: One Day, One Decade.* London: Preface.
2. "I had called Dylan through..." ~ Geldof, Bob. (1988). *Is That it?* New York: Ballantine.
3. "crass, stupid and nationalistic" ~ Geldof, Bob. (1988). *Is That it?* New York: Ballantine.
4. "We spent a week rehearsing..." ~ Goldberg, Michael. (1986, January 16). Back on the road. *Rolling Stone.*
5. "There was nobody in the..." ~ George-Warren, Holly (Ed.). (2005). *Farm Aid: A Song for America.* New York: Rodale.
6. "When we went to the..." ~ Goldberg, Michael. (1986, January 16). Back on the road. *Rolling Stone.*
7. "Live Aid and Farm Aid..." ~ Gilmore, Mikal. (1985, October 13). Behind the glasses, Dylan at 44 looking scruffy but ready. *The Los Angeles Herald-Examiner.*

CHAPTER 2: DYLAN & THE HEARTBREAKERS:
1. "Are you kidding? Put me..." ~ Goldberg, Michael. (1986, January 16). Back on the road. *Rolling Stone.*
2. "I was a little nervous..." ~ Rowland, Mark. (1987, September). Heartbreaker straight ahead. *Musician.*
3. "[Dylan would say], 'Here's the..." ~ Bream, Jon. (1986, June 22). The many faces of Bob Dylan. *The (Minneapolis-St.Paul) Star Tribune.*
4. "after the under-rehearsed band..." ~ DeCurtis, Anthony. (1986, March 27). Dylan down under. *Rolling Stone.*
5. "According to some reviews, the..." ~ Gilmore, Mikal. (1986, July 17). Positively Dylan. *Rolling Stone.*
6. "I got to sing 'Knockin...'" ~ White, Timothy. (1990). *Rock Lives.* New York: Henry Holt and Company.

7. While in New Zealand, Bob... ~ Sounes, Howard. (2001). *Down the Highway: The Life of Bob Dylan.* New York: Grove Press.

8. "Everyone's always saying to me..." ~ Gilmore, Mikal. (1986, July 17). Positively Dylan. *Rolling Stone.*

9. "As a matter of fact..." ~ Flanagan, Bill. (1986, April). Tom Petty pulls together: The Southern soul of a Hollywood rocker. *Musician.*

10. "It's a sure bet that..." ~ Tucker, Ken. (1986, July 21). Music: Dylan and Petty at Spectrum. *The Philadelphia Inquirer.*

11. "one of the most forgettable..." ~ Sounes, Howard. (2001). *Down the Highway: The Life of Bob Dylan.* New York: Grove Press.

12. "If the audience wanted a..." ~ Taylor, Jonathon. (1986, June 15). Bob Dylan plus Tom Petty adds up to tour de force for concert. *The Chicago Tribune.*

13. "Garcia had attended a Dylan-Petty..." ~ Jackson, Blair. (2000). *Garcia: An American Life.* New York: Penguin.

CHAPTER 3: THE CLOSE OF THE DYLAN / PETTY TOUR:

1. "I took Dylan to see..." ~ Flanagan, Bill. (1990, April). The Heartbreakers highway. *Musician.*

2. "For the next few concerts..." ~ Maymudes, Victor & Maymudes, Jacob. (2016). *Another Side of Bob Dylan.* New York: St. Martin's Press.

3. "In these first four shows..." ~ Dylan, Bob, (2004). *Chronicles: Volume One.* New York: Simon & Schuster.

4. "There are a hundred requests..." ~ Shain, Britta Lee. (2016). *Seeing The Real You At Last.* London: Jawbone Press.

5. "We were pretty worn out..." ~ Uhelszki, Jaan. (2012, June). Tom Petty: Won't back down. *Uncut.*

6. "I just thought, okay, it's..." ~ Simmons, Sylvie. (2006, October). Rock of ages. *Mojo.*

7. "By the time we got..." ~ Hilburn, Robert. (1987, May 24). A Petty mood: A classic rocker's passion is refreshed. *The Los Angeles Times.*

8. "I'd been on an eighteen..." ~ Dylan, Bob, (2004). *Chronicles: Volume One.* New York: Simon & Schuster.

9. "Being an enigma at 20..." ~ Peel, John. (2004, October 30). 'The music was dogmatic and humourless.' *The Guardian.*

CHAPTER 4: CROSSING PATHS: GEORGE, TOM & ROY:

1. "I first met him in..." ~ Udovitch, Mim; & Wild, David. (2002, January 17). Remembering George. *Rolling Stone.*

2. "I reminded him that we'd..." ~ Udovitch, Mim; & Wild, David. (2002, January 17). Remembering George. *Rolling Stone.*

3. "They came out and just..." ~ Bosso, Joe. (2004, May). American idols. *Guitar World.*

4. "I went back to L.A..." ~ Udovitch, Mim; & Wild, David. (2002, January 17). Remembering George. *Rolling Stone.*

5. "We weren't even thinking about..." ~ Zimmer, Dave. (1989, May 5). Once in a full moon. *BAM.*

6. And according to one of... ~ *The Jim Bohannon Show.* (2014, May 22). Interview with Roy Orbison, Jr. Dial Global Network.

7. "I agreed because I was..." ~ Nash, Jesse. (1989, November). Roy Orbison. *Music Express.*

8. "when Roy started to go..." ~ Amburn, Ellis. (1990). *Dark Star: The Roy Orbison Story.* New York: Carol Publishing Group.

9. "Roy Orbison was the only... " ~ Orbison, Roy. (2008). *The Soul of Rock and Roll* [booklet]. Monument / Orbison Records / Legacy.

10. "His songs had songs within..." ~ Dylan, Bob, (2004). *Chronicles: Volume One.* New York: Simon & Schuster.

11. "The people who walked out..." ~ Shelton, Robert. (2011). *No Direction Home: The Life and Music of Bob Dylan.* Milwaukee: Hal Leonard Corporation.

12. "Hey – I got an idea..." ~ Robertson, Robbie. (2016). *Testimony.* New York: Crown Archetype.

13. "George, in his late twenties..." ~ Shapiro, Marc. (2005). *All Things Must Pass: The Life of George Harrison.* London: Virgin.

14. "He was Bob's biggest fan..." ~ The Editors of *Rolling Stone.* (2012). *Harrison.* New York: Simon and Schuster.

15. "It was a day I'll..." ~ Sounes, Howard. (2001). *Down the Highway: The Life of Bob Dylan.* New York: Grove Press.

CHAPTER 5: THE BEATLES SPAWN ELO:

1. "I went into the studio there..." ~ Mehr, Bob, (2016, December). From Shard End to Beverly Hills, Jeff Lynne. *Mojo.*

2. "Between 1972 and 1986, ELO..." ~ Yarborough, Chuck. (2017, March 31). Electric Light Orchestra. *The Cleveland Plain Dealer.*

3. "I first met Bob [Dylan]..." ~ Bonner, Michael. (2016, April). An audience with... Jeff Lynne. *Uncut.*

4. "If I could've picked one..." ~ DeCurtis, Anthony. (1987, October 22). George Harrison gets back. *Rolling Stone.*

5. "George said, 'I'm thinking about..." ~ Jackson, Blair. (2011, December). Classic tracks: George Harrison's 'Got My Mind Set On You.' *Mix.*

6. "Jeff was accordingly invited to..." ~ Kiste, John Van Der. (2015). *Jeff Lynne: The Electric Light Orchestra Before and After.* London: Fonthill Media.

7. "Lynne was the strongest personality..." ~ Leng, Simon. (2006). *While My Guitar Gently Weeps: The Music of George Harrison.* Milwaukee, WI: Hal Leonard.

8. "and the Traveling Wilburys project..." ~ Leng, Simon. (2006). *While My Guitar Gently Weeps: The Music of George Harrison.* Milwaukee, WI: Hal Leonard.

9. "We were three-quarters of..." ~ Scopa, Bud. (2007, September). The inside story of the Traveling Wilburys: Rock's greatest ever supergroup. *Uncut.*

10. "George wasn't seeking a career..." ~ Hiatt, Brian. (2011, September 15). The private life of George Harrison. *Rolling Stone.*

CHAPTER 6: TOM PETTY & JEFF LYNNE:

1. "well, he doesn't do outside..." ~ Sharp, Ken. (2013, January). The dream team. *Goldmine.*

2. "We started playing around at..." ~ Zimmer, Dave. (1989, May 5). Once in a full moon. *BAM.*

3. "I remember coming home with..." ~ Sharp, Ken. (2013, January). The dream team. *Goldmine.*

4. "He was very nervous about..." ~ Corcoran, Michael. (1989, August). Raised on promises. *Spin.*

5. "While they were mixing [the..." ~ Sharp, Ken. (2013, January). The dream team. *Goldmine.*

6. "All the songs were written..." ~ Morse, Steve. (1989, May 4). Tom Petty's year off wasn't to be. *The Boston Globe.*

CHAPTER 7: ROY ORBISON MAKES A COMEBACK:

1. "So [Jeff Lynne] had Roy..." ~ Zimmer, Dave. (1989, May 5). Once in a full moon. *BAM.*
2. "The first time I heard..." ~ Orbison, Roy. (2008). *The Soul of Rock and Roll* [booklet]. Monument / Orbison Records / Legacy.
3. "Written in Christmas '87, before..." ~ Kruth, John. (2013). *Rhapsody in Black: The Life and Music of Roy Orbison.* Milwaukee, WI: BackBeat Books.
4. "is a warmly hopeful greeting..." ~ Silverma, David. (1989, February 2). Orbison's 'Mystery Girl' is a poignant comeback. *The Chicago Tribune.*
5. "In the mid-80s he told..." ~ Black, Johnny. (2008, October). Roy Orbison. *Music Week.*
6. "It is a beautiful song..." ~ Lehman, Peter (2003). *Roy Orbison: The Invention of an Alternative Rock Masculinity.* Philadelphia: Temple University Press.
7. "Put into rotation as a..." ~ Sachs, Lloyd. (2016*). T Bone Burnett: A Life in Pursuit.* Austin: University of Texas Press.
8 ."My mom and dad wanted..." ~ Ruggiero, Bob. (2017, March 24). Roy Orbison's sons help refresh his 'Black & White Night.' *The Houston Press.*
9. "What riles me about *Laminar*..." ~ Marsh, Dave. (1979, August 23). Roy Orbison: Laminar Flow. *Rolling Stone.*

CHAPTER 8: GEORGE HARRISON NEEDS A B-SIDE:

1. "He was seated at a table..." ~ DeCurtis, Anthony. (2002, January 17). After the Beatles. *Rolling Stone.*
2. "George was very smooth. He..." ~ Hurwitz, Matt. (2007, June 11). Wilburys set to travel again. *USA Today.*
3. "I drove Jeff down there..." ~ Jones, Allan; & Love, Damien. (2014, August). What good am I? *Uncut.*
4. "Tom called me down to..." ~ Guerra, Tom. (2008, March). Mike Campbell. *ToneQuest Report.*
5. "'Handle With Care' was finished..." ~ Scoppa, Bud. (2007, September). The inside story of the Traveling Wilburys. *Uncut.*
6. "The record company said, 'Oh..." ~ Rowland, Mark. (1990, March). The quiet Wilbury. *Musician.*
7. "What starts as a typically..." ~ Staunton, Terry. (2007, July). Traveling Wilburys: The Traveling Wilbury Collection. *Record Collector.*
8. The five men soon celebrated... ~ Rodman, Sarah. (2015, November 19). All you need to know about Tom Petty. *The Boston Globe.*
9. "We all jumped in a..." ~ Zimmer, Dave. (1989, May 5). Once in a full moon. *BAM.*
10. "[George] and Jeff used to..." ~ Hurwitz, Matt. (2007, June 11). Wilburys set to travel again. *USA Today.*
11. "We didn't ask any of..." ~ Ashton, Martin. (1989, February 24). Last testament, blue angel, *BAM.*
12. "Tom Petty came down and..." ~ Stewart, Dave. (2008). *The Dave Stewart Songbook: The Stories Behind the Songs, Volume One.* Encinitas, CA: Surfdog.
13. "He said to Jimmy, 'I..." ~ Stewart, Dave. (2008). *The Dave Stewart Songbook: The Stories Behind the Songs, Volume One.* Encinitas, CA: Surfdog.
14. "The reason why I built..." ~ Zanes, Warren (Ed.). (2005). *Runnin' Down a Dream: Tom Petty and the Heartbreakers.* San Francisco: Chronicle Books.
15. "I'd agreed to produce Feargal..." ~ Stewart, Dave. (2016). *Sweet Dreams Are Made of This.* New York: New American Library.

16. "Bob Dylan had told me..." ~ Stewart, Dave. (2016). *Sweet Dreams are Made of This*. New York: New American Library.
17. "I built that house from..." ~ Rodman, Sarah. (2016, February 9). Eurythmics' Dave Stewart recalls 'Sweet Dreams' of his long career. *The Boston Globe*.
18. "It was kind of weird..." ~ Stewart, Dave. (2008). *The Dave Stewart Songbook: The Stories Behind the Songs, Volume One*. Encinitas, CA: Surfdog.
19. "I think everybody was kind..." ~ Mehr, Bob, (2016, December). From Shard End to Beverly Hills, Jeff Lynne... *Mojo*.
20. "George was kind of the..." ~ Thomson, Graeme. (2015). *George Harrison: Behind the Locked Door*. New York: Overlook Omnibus.
21. "Well, they treated me equally..." ~ di Perna, Alan. (1999, April). Tom Petty: American boy. *Pulse*.
22. "We got everyone to agree..." ~ Rowland, Mark. (1990, March). The quiet Wilbury. *Musician*.
23. "We'd start out every day..." ~ Scopa, Bud. (2007, September). The inside story of the Traveling Wilburys: Rock's greatest ever supergroup. *Uncut*.
24. "Outside of writing with the..." ~ Zollo, Paul. (1991, no. 16). Bob Dylan: The *Song Talk* Interview. *Song Talk*.
25. "In almost every song, however..." ~ Rockwell, John. (1988, November 13). Old Timers Out for a Spin Cut a Couple of Disks. *The New York Times*.
26. "We usually went by a..." ~ Rowland, Mark. (1990, March). The quiet Wilbury. *Musician*.
27. Harrison would describe Crisp as... ~ Greene, Joshua M. (2006). *Here Comes the Sun: The Spiritual and Musical Journey of George Harrison*. Hoboken, NJ: John Wiley & Sons.
28. "There was no room in..." ~ Wright, Gary. (2014). *Dream Weaver: A Memoir*. New York: Penguin.
29. "It's this new group I..." ~ Coburn, Bob. (1988, February 10). George Harrison. *Rockline*.

CHAPTER 9: VOLUME ONE:

1. "Their 'anonymity' is just pretense..." ~ Rockwell, John. (1988, November 13). Old Timers Out for a Spin Cut a Couple of Disks. *The New York Times*.
2. "This is the best record..." ~ Wild, David. (1988, December 1). Here comes the fun. *Rolling Stone*.
3. "It may not prove to..." ~ Morse, Steve. (1987, October 23). 'Traveling Wilburys' offers absurdist fun. *The Boston Globe*.
4. "I'll never forget being in..." ~ Black, Johnny. (2008, October). Roy Orbison. *Music Week*.
5. "'Tweeter And The Monkey Man'..." ~ The Traveling Wilburys. (1990). *The Traveling Wilburys*. Guildford, Surrey, England: Genesis Publications.
6. "When Roy came to sing..." ~ Goldberg, Michael; Ressner, Jeffrey; & Pond, Steve [Compilers]. (1989, January 26). Tributes. *Rolling Stone*.
7. "Though we've all said we'd..." ~ Holden, Stephen. (1988, November 24). Traveling Wilburys turn accident into hit record. *The Chicago Tribune*.

CHAPTER 10: PETTY: SONGS FROM THE GARAGE:

1. "I think there was some..." ~ Mitchell, Rick. (1989, July 9). Veteran rocker has never sounded better. *The Houston Chronicle*.

2. "[Benmont Tench] used to say..." ~ Holan, Marc. (1991, September 6). A conversation with Tom Petty. *Scene.*
3. "It's the only time in..." ~ Newman, Melinda. (2005, December 3). Tom Petty: A portrait of the artist. *Billboard.*
4. "I carried a tape around..." ~ Gundersen, Edna. (1990, February 9). Petty at his peak. *USA Today.*
5. "We had Tom Petty on..." ~ Moseley, Willie G. (2002, October). Chris Hillman: Bluegrass, bass, and back again. *Vintage Guitar.*
6. "My daughter thought I wrote..." ~ DeYoung, Bill. (1989, April 26). Tom Petty presents a solo album. *The Gainesville Sun.*
7. "*Full Moon Fever* isn't Petty's..." ~ Guterman, Jimmy. (1989, May 4). Tom Petty's solo effort: An infectious 'fever.' *Rolling Stone.*
8. "My life changed, the whole..." ~ Schruers, Fred. (1995, May 4). Tom Petty on the road: This is how it feels. *Rolling Stone.*
9. "The album seemed a turning..." ~ Simmons, Sylvie. (1989, June 14). Moonlighting. *Raw.*
10. "It was sort of deliberate..." ~ Simmons, Sylvie. (1989, June 14). Moonlighting. *Raw.*
11. "acoustic wall of sound..." ~ Dye, Robert; & Trost, Isaiah. (2003, March 10). Rock and roll animals. *Guitar World Acoustic.*
12. "a deeply inspired, very Harrison-esque..." ~ Aledort, Andy. (1995, August). Chartbreaker. *Guitar School.*
13. "It was George's idea to..." ~ Fricke, David. (2009, December 10). It's good to be king. *Rolling Stone.*
14. The track would set a... ~ Whitburn, Joel. (2008). *Rock Tracks 1981-2008.* Menomonee Falls, WI: Record Research.
15. "That was the first time..." ~ Wild, David. (1991, August 8). Over the hump. *Rolling Stone.*
16. "For the first time in..." ~ Wild, David. (1991, August 8). Over the hump. *Rolling Stone.*
17. "The Heartbreakers want to stay..." ~ Flanagan, Bill. (1990, April). The Heartbreakers highway. *Musician.*
18. "We don't have any plans..." ~ Holan, Mark. (1989, June 8). Of full moons and Wilburys. *Scene.*
19. "I've always played around in..." ~ "Reclusive George Harrison on the road again." (1992, July 16). *The Baltimore Sun.*
20. "A lot of money was..." ~ Wild, David. (1991, August 8). Over the hump. *Rolling Stone.*
21. "promoters kept calling and calling" ~ Flanagan, Bill. (1990, April). The Heartbreakers highway. *Musician.*

CHAPTER 11: ROY ORBISON: IN DREAMS:

1. "At first glance, it seems..." ~ Heim, Chris. (1988, March 30). Rock pioneer Roy Orbison shows he can still wow 'em. *The Chicago Tribune.*
2. "I've been rediscovered by young..." ~ Duffy, Thom. (1988, December 8). Rock 'n' roll pioneer Roy Orbison dies. *The Orlando Sentinel.*
3. "talked about intensive rehearsals in..." ~ Ruggiero, Bob. (2017, March 24). Roy Orbison's sons help refresh his 'Black & White Night.' *The Houston Press.*
4. "Wesley had spoken to his..." ~ Jerome, Jim. (1988, December 19). Bard of the lonely. *People.*

5. "Mr. Orbison gave a concert..." ~ Pareles, Jon. (1988, December 8). Roy Orbison, 52, a singer famed for plaintive pop anthems, dies. *The New York Times*.
6. "The way Roy saw life..." ~ Zimmer, Dave. (1989, May 5). Once in a full moon. *BAM*.
7. "I always felt like he..." ~ Lanham, Tom. (1994, December). Petty on the inside. *Pulse*.
8. "That was devastating because it..." ~ Cole, Paul. (2014, March 13). ELO legend Jeff Lynne: I would not have liked being in The Beatles. *The Birmingham Mail*.
9. "People seem to dwell on..." ~ Wilde, Jon. (1989, February). Roy Orbison: The Big O. *Blitz*.
10. "I was lucky. Without immediate..." ~ Jerome, Jim. (1979, June 18). Going disco is no sweat after Roy Orbison's earlier survival test: heart surgery. *People*.
11. "'Make sure it's a clean..." ~ Jerome, Jim. (1979, June 18). Going disco is no sweat after Roy Orbison's earlier survival test: heart surgery. *People*.
12. "Roy's father, Orbie Lee had..." ~ Kruth, John. (2013). *Rhapsody in Black: The Life and Music of Roy Orbison*. Milwaukee, WI: BackBeat Books.
13. "felt healthy" and responded, "Yeah..." ~ Pond, Steve. (1989, January 26). Roy Orbison: 1936-1988. *Rolling Stone*.

CHAPTER 12: RETURN OF THE TRAVELING WILBURYS:
1. "There was a deep and..." ~ Jones, Allan. (2008, November). Life with Bob Dylan, 1989-2006. *Uncut*.
2. "would do double duty as..." ~ Brodie, John; & Kamp, Jason. (1990, December). Building a better Wilbury. *Spy*.
3. "You can't replace Roy Orbison..." ~ Rowland, Mark. (1990, March). The quiet Wilbury. *Musician*.
4. "I was in LA busy..." ~ Thomson, Graeme. (2015). *George Harrison: Behind the Locked Door*. New York: Overlook Omnibus.

CHAPTER 13: RECORDING THE SECOND ALBUM:
1. "That was George's idea..." ~ Hurwitz, Matt. (2007, June 11). Wilburys set to travel again. *USA Today*.
2. "For the second album they..." ~ Maymudes, Victor & Maymudes, Jacob. (2016). *Another Side of Bob Dylan*. New York: St. Martin's Press.
3. "People don't listen to records..." ~ Rowland, Mark. (1997, January). Beck meets Petty: Rockin', writin', survivin' in L.A. *Musician*.
4. "We just set up in the..." ~ Henke, James. (1990, October 4). The second coming of Jeff Lynne. *Rolling Stone*.
5. "We all throw in ideas..." ~ The second coming of Jeff Lynne. *Rolling Stone*.
6. "There's no telling what kind..." ~ Gundersen, Edna. (1990, November 7). On 'Vol. 3,' the Traveling Wilburys enjoy the ride. *USA Today*.
7. "It was Roy's presence [that]..." ~ Sounes, Howard. (2001). *Down the Highway: The Life of Bob Dylan*. New York: Grove Press.
8. "Last time, it was a..." ~ Gundersen, Edna. (1990, November 7). On 'Vol. 3,' the Traveling Wilburys enjoy the ride. *USA Today*.
9. "[it] stays close to 1950's..." ~ Pareles, Jon. (1990, November 4). Shake, rattle and growing old with the Wilburys. *The New York Times*.
10. "Inevitably, the album lacks the..." ~ McLeese Don. (1990. November 29). Vol. 3: Traveling Wilburys. *Rolling Stone*.
11. "The first song we wrote..." ~ The Traveling Wilburys. (1990). *The Traveling Wilburys*. Guildford, Surrey, England: Genesis Publications.

12. "we going over Niagra Falls..." ~ "The Traveling Wilburys." (1990). *Nightbeat.*
13. "it's too tiring.... it's not..." ~ "The Traveling Wilburys." (1990). *Nightbeat.*
14. "George had some wacky ideas..." ~ Greene, Andy. (2016, January 28). My life in 10 songs: Jeff Lynne. *Rolling Stone.*

CHAPTER 14: ALL THINGS MUST PASS:

1. "I think it was probably..." ~ Sharp, Ken. (2013, January). The dream team. *Goldmine.*
2. "They dug Jeff. It was..." ~ Ressner. Jeffrey. (1991. October). Tom Petty: Traveling Heartbreaker. *CD Review.*
3. "Maybe it was a case..." ~ Flanagan, Bill. (1994, November). Into the great wide open. *Mojo.*
4. "full of hazy references, half-baked..." ~ Racine, Marty. (1991, June 30). Mediocrity from Tom Petty. *The Houston Chronicle.*
5. "[Eric] and George were pals..." ~ [Phantom, Slim Jim. (2016). *A Stray Cat Struts: My Life as a Rockabilly Rebel.* New York: Thomas Dunne Books.
6. "It's so loud and smokey... " ~ Udovitch, Mim; & Wild, David. (2002, January 17). Remembering George. *Rolling Stone.*
7. "I was worried. He's such..." ~ Snow, Mat. (1995, November). Paul McCartney. *Mojo.*
8. "They spent the first day..." ~ Lynskey, Dorian. (2015, November 14). Return of the hitman. *Billboard.*
9. "I've just let go of..." ~ Hiatt, Brian. (2011, September 15). The private life of George Harrison. *Rolling Stone.*
10. "I spoke to Ringo about..." ~ Doggett, Peter. (2010). *You Never Give Me Your Money.* New York: Harper.
11. "The man certainly wasn't auditioning..." ~ DeCurtis, Anthony. (2002, January 17). After the Beatles. *Rolling Stone.*
12. "I was mostly just amazed..." ~ Thompson, Art. (2006, July). The heart of the matter: Mike Campbell on crafting the Heartbreakers' guitar sounds. *Guitar Player.*
13. "We never thought we were..." ~ Hiatt, Brian. (2011, September 15). The private life of George Harrison. *Rolling Stone.*
14. "My daughter Adria used to..." ~ Petty, Tom. (2002, January 17). Remembering George. *Rolling Stone.*
15. "In the spring of 2002..." ~ Clapton, Eric. (2007). *Clapton: The Autobiography.* New York: Broadway Books.
16. "In the afternoon, Dhani came..." ~ Harris. (1992, January 23). All-star tribute to George Harrison. *Rolling Stone.*
17. "It wasn't the first time..." ~ Fraser, Graham. (2002, November 9). Harrison's guitar gently weeps again: Former Beatle's pal Jeff Lynne produces posthumous CD. *The Toronto Star.*
18. "It was so depressing, as..." ~ Bonner, Michael. (2016, April). An audience with... Jeff Lynne. *Uncut.*
19. "I've been a real control..." ~ Gundersen, Edna. (2001, November 22). It's all right: Harrison's son completes dad's last album. *USA Today.*
20 "Much of the material deals..." ~ Fraser, Graham. (2002, November 9). Harrison's guitar gently weeps again: Former Beatle's pal Jeff Lynne produces posthumous CD. *The Toronto Star.*
21. "The rhythm of the wind..." ~ The Editors of *Rolling Stone.* (2012). *Harrison.* New York: Simon and Schuster.

CHAPTER 15: AFTER THE WILBURYS:

1. "The Traveling Wilburys' album was..." ~ Azerrad, Michael; DeCurtis, Anthony; Fricke, David; et al. (1989, November 16). The 100 best albums of the eighties. *Rolling Stone.*

2. "George really wanted to do..." ~ Endelman, Michael. (2005, December 2). What ever happened to the Traveling Wilburys? *Entertainment Weekly.*

3. What ever happened to the... ~ Endelman, Michael. (2005, December 2). What ever happened to the Traveling Wilburys? *Entertainment Weekly.*

4. "They were completed, except for..." ~ Hurwitz, Matt. (2007, June 11). Wilburys set to travel again. *USA Today.*

5. "Brainwashed starts with a jaunty..." ~ Bauder, David. (2002, November 14). Posthumous Harrison album is stunning. *The Alton Telegraph.*

6. "The performance went well, so..." ~ Thompson, Art. (2006, July). 30 years & counting. *Guitar Player.*

7. "It's not a real loud..." ~ Gundersen, Edna. (2006, July 25). Tom Petty concert news and tickets. *USA Today.*

8. "Lately I've been concerned with..." ~ Uhelszki, Jaan. (2006, July/August). Tom Petty: Anatomy of a rockstar. *Harp.*

9. "We left his house pinching..." ~ Millicia, Joe. (2006, July 5). Rock Hall pays tribute to Tom Petty. *The Akron Beacon Journal.*

10. "I think the first records..." ~ Hunter, James. (2000). In Barbara Schultz (Ed.), *Music Producers: Conversations with Today's Top Hitmakers.* Emeryville, CA: MixBooks.

11. "I met in 1971, in..." ~ Mehr, Bob, (2016, December). From Shard End to Beverly Hills, Jeff Lynne. *Mojo.*

12. "I was a great collaborator..." ~ Lynskey, Dorian. (2015, November 14). Return of the hitman. *Billboard.*

13. "Do I regret not touring..." ~ Bonner, Michael. (2016, April). An audience with... Jeff Lynne. *Uncut.*

14. "I've been incredibly lucky. I've..." ~ Sandall, Robert. (2007, February). Jeff Lynne: 'I've worked with The Beatles and Dylan. I've lived every fan's dream. *Q.*

15. "He had a great thing..." ~ Rodman, Sarah. (2011, June 28). Chris Isaak's 5 favorite Sun recording artists. *The Boston Globe.*

16. "[In 1989] I had two..." ~ Dylan, Bob, (2004). *Chronicles: Volume One.* New York: Simon & Schuster.]

17. "Are the Traveling Wilburys Rock..." ~ Smith, Troy L. (2017, March 28. Are the Traveling Wilburys Rock & Roll Hall of Fame worthy? *The Cleveland Plain Dealer.*

18. "Frankly, were it not for..." ~ Yarborough, Chuck. (2017, April 2). Electric Light Orchestra. *The Cleveland Plain Dealer.*

19. "It's such a shame that..." ~ Fitzpatrick, Rob. (2009, November 15). New Tom Petty album *The Live Anthology. The Times of London.*

20. "Could we do it again..." ~ Cole, Paul. (2014, March 13). ELO legend Jeff Lynne: I would not have liked being in The Beatles. *The Birmingham Mail.*

21. "It's shocking, crushing news. I..." ~ Lewis, Randy. (2017, October 3). Tom Petty, Heartbreakers frontman and beloved rock figure, dies at 66. *The Los Angeles Times.*

22. "This year has been a..." ~ Lewis, Randy. (2017, October 4). Tom Petty's final interview: There was supposed to have been so much more. *The Los Angeles Times.*

EPILOGUE:

1. "felt like there was some..." ~ Erickson, Steve. (2008, June). Time stops for no one. *Relix*.

▶ INDEX

Universal Sound Stage, 8
University of Illinois Memorial
Stadium, 7
U2, 48, 75

V

Van Halen, 45
Veale, Eddie, 63
Vee, Bobby, 27
Vela, Rosie, 124
Ventura Theatre, 72
VH1, 108
Virgin Records, 47, 55

W

Waldorf Astoria, 46, 115
Wallace, Ian, 59
Walsh, Joe, 3, 104, 125
Warner Brothers Records, 34, 49,
55, 65, 96
Waronker, Lenny, 52, 96
Was, Don, 87-88
Watts, Charlie, 109
Weidel, Alan "Bugs," 59, 118
Westlake Recording Studios, 52
White, Barry, 88
The White Album, 32
Wilbury, Ayrton, 118
Wilbury, Boo, 93
Wilbury, Charles Truscott, Sr.,
65
Wilbury, Charlie T., Jr., 66
Wilbury, Clayton, 93
Wilbury, Ken, 98
Wilbury, Lefty, 66, 93
Wilbury, Lucky, 66, 105
Wilbury, Muddy, 93
Wilbury, Nelson, 66, 104
Wilbury, Otis, 66
Wilbury, Spike, 93, 104

Wilbury Mountain Studio, 94
Williams, Hank, (Sr.), 8
Wilson, Brian, 25
Winwood, Steve, 115
WMCA (New York), 21
WNEW (New York), 32
Wood, Ronnie, 7, 14
Wright, Gary, 37, 49, 62, 113

Y

Young, Neil, 8, 105

Z

Zoom, 123
Zwan, 2

CPSIA information can be obtained
at www.ICGtesting.com
Printed in the USA
BVHW040309171020
591031BV00011B/779

9 780980 056174